DOMESTIC ABUSE, CHILD CUSTODY, AND VISITATION

DOMESTIC ABUSE, CHILD CUSTODY, AND VISITATION

Winning in Family Court

Toby G. Kleinman

AND

Daniel Pollack

OXFORD
UNIVERSITY PRESS

OXFORD
UNIVERSITY PRESS

Oxford University Press is a department of the University of Oxford. It furthers
the University's objective of excellence in research, scholarship, and education
by publishing worldwide. Oxford is a registered trade mark of Oxford University
Press in the UK and certain other countries.

Published in the United States of America by Oxford University Press
198 Madison Avenue, New York, NY 10016, United States of America.

© Toby G. Kleinman and Daniel Pollack 2017

CIP data is on file at the Library of Congress
ISBN 978–0–19–064157–3

3 5 7 9 8 6 4 2

Printed by Sheridan Books, Inc., United States of America

To Robert Adler, my Partner in life and my partner in law,
whose love and support I can always count on.
To Rivka Rachel Pollack, my wife for life.

CONTENTS

CONTENTS

PREFACE

Tears stream down my face as I stop the car to make the phone call, my heart racing. My instincts tell me not to stop. I left because I was forced to leave, and my instincts tell me not to call home now. I am certain that if I call I will feel worse. Yet I feel an intense pressure to speak to "Him." I try to assess the situation. I'm glad I'm gone, yet I'm frightened because I had finally been so provoked that I actually left. I made many threats in the past ten years. I finally carried one out.

This afternoon feels different somehow.

I know I am really leaving for good, not just for the weekend. I cannot recount the number of times I'd felt like leaving. But today, I actually packed a suitcase, put the children in the car, and made my exit. Why then am I feeling so confused now? Why am I having so much difficulty driving the car? I know I have been unhappy for a long time. I know "He" has also been unhappy. Can I not stand to risk being rejected if I call? Will I run back out of fear? It makes no sense. Is everything I am feeling just based on economics because I believe "His" lie that I am incapable of sustaining myself and my three children?

Randy and Ramona are asleep in the car. David, eight years old, is asking me if I am sad. I mumble something that is barely audible. I can hardly see to drive through my tears. Of course, David knows I am unhappy. Of course, he knows there is trouble between his father and me. But he did not witness the scene this time. At least I feel good about that. This morning I behaved like a crazy person. Was I crazy? I feel a tremendous pressure in my head, as if an explosion is about to take place inside my brain. I must relieve the pressure. In an attempt to feel better, I stop the car. I make the call. There is no answer. The pressure is building. My guilt is rising. Did He have another heart attack?

I get back on the road. I am driving to Woodbury. I have a destination! That is different from the past. I never told anyone. This time I called my parents. I called right away. I called when my insides felt like ripping apart. I know that if I did not call, then I would not go. "Be involved," I said out loud to myself. "Call your mother," I urged myself. Tell her you have a rotten son-of-a-bitch husband. Tell her you need help. Tell her you want to run away from yourself. Tell her that if you stay another day, you will do something drastic.

I have got to protect the children. You can throw your own life away, but you do not have the right to destroy the children. They will be destroyed if you stay.

This morning I shouted at him, "David is unhappy and depressed. Randy is a mess. He is starting to stutter and stammer with you!" I screamed at him, "Ramona is such a tiny baby. I can spare her if I leave now."

With that, I had called my mother in Woodbury to ask if I could come for the weekend for which she had previously invited us. Even as I called, I wondered if I had the right to leave. Maybe I am the source of all the kids' ills. Maybe my unhappiness is all my fault. After all, I had started the scene this morning. It was I who woke up ready to fight. "I hate you," I had said to Him. "You are so mean and selfish. How long can I continue to fight you? How long can I continue to prove to you that I am a good person? Why is it that I can never do enough for you? Why is everything always my fault, yet I always feel sorry for you?"

As I feel the anger now, my tears subside. I tell myself that he loves me. I tell myself that he will realize how terrific I am and beg me to come back. But I know better. I know I will, in the end, feel sorry for "Him." I will, in the end, apologize for having hurt his feelings, though he destroyed mine. People will think that I am the strong-willed one and that "He" is meek and giving. That is the image he forced me into creating. I have been living the lie for so long now, it almost feels like me. I must break that lie.

I have only driven a few short miles in the hour I have been driving. I think I should turn back. The little ones won't know the difference. Randy has never been to my parents' country house in Woodbury in his three-and one-half years. David tells me about the fun he is going to have when he gets there. He enumerates all the things he loves about Woodbury. They all involve Grandpa—my father. I feel glad that David has experienced the love of my father. He has had glimpses of generosity and love from a man. He has seen that a man can really care.

I feel that I must go on, but I am not sure if I can. I cannot stop crying. Again the pressure in my head mounts. I cannot stop the pain. I know I would end up crazy if I stayed. Why, then, am I having so much trouble leaving? It makes no sense. He was always angry with me. He was always angry with the kids. I was always trying to prove to him that he had no reason to be angry. I was always trying to prove my worth to him. He was constantly denigrating my family, my roots. He always was so certain that he knew everyone's motives for their behavior. I had swallowed that lie for so long.

Even as I drive I continue to ask if he is right. Are my parents awful people? I hate myself for even asking. It has always been the knowledge that I could count on them that has sustained me in the past, when

I was hurt. I feel grateful that they never gave up on me, that they still love me. I even suspect they have an idea of the pain I have been living with, the isolation and the desolation. I know they will help if I can only get there. I stop the car again. David wonders why I keep calling. I mumble another answer. My eyes are so puffy I can barely see. I finally know that I can't drive anymore.

Woodbury may take me four more hours at this rate. But if I turn around, I'll be home in an hour. I turn off the road. There is a gas station. I leave the kids in the car. I make the call. As the phone rings, I can already hear the tension in "His" voice. I hear a quiet "hello." I slur over apologies for starting a fight this morning. He is cold. "I am not the same person I was when you left me an hour ago," he tells me. "I took a walk to the post office after you left. I felt free, Tammy. I feel terrific." Rejection! I knew it! I feared it! I start to say that I'll go back anyway. I'll show him I am a good person.

I'll show him that he is free with me as a wife. I force myself, instead, to say goodbye.

First, I had better call Dad and tell him I am not coming. After all, I am expected. I dial the number but there is no answer. Why are they not home when they expect me shortly? I remind myself that I want to go home. I decide I had better keep driving until I reach Dad. I urge myself on.

I drive onto the highway. The scenery is a blank to me. I try to stop the tears, but they continue to flow as the pain of the rejection smarts.

He feels good. I replay our conversation. I feel agony, and "He" feels good. As always! He is always happiest when I hurt. I wonder why I stayed so long. He has never really shared any joy with me. He is selfish. He is arbitrary.

He is incessantly angry and full of wrath toward the world around him. I decide to continue in the same direction. The tears are worse than ever. David expresses concern. Randy wakes up and so does Ramona.

I am not certain if I can drive any longer. Randy is cranky. David tries to entertain him. David tells Randy how much fun Woodbury is.

I feel like I must turn around. My head is pounding! I can hear my heart thumping in my ears. The noise is crushing. That awful place in the mountains. I hate it there! Certain I can drive no more, I stop the car again. I find a station and I call "Him." There is no answer. I had better call Dad and tell him I am going back "home." I get an operator and put my call through. It seems to be taking forever. The phone rings and rings and rings. Finally, "Hello." "Dad—I don't know what to do. I can hardly drive." "Keep coming, Tammy" he says. "Drive slowly and carefully." He reassures me that it will take only a little longer that way. "You might as well come, since you are on the way." He is so cool and calm. Maybe I am imagining the pain I am in. But he says to come, so I will. I feel like a robot with no mind of my own. If "He" had answered and asked me to come home, would I have listened to him? I reflect on my parents' invitation to visit the country. It was so timely. I had refused at first. But this morning I just could not bear the pressure any longer. I had called to accept the invitation, but I had said nothing about our fight. I merely accepted an invitation to visit. I am not even certain they know. I am leaving "Him" and leaving the marriage. I really must be cracking up. I feel relieved, as if I needed someone to make a decision for me. I must get away from him. I must get my life back together. I have three little children who need protection from that man. The children need a sane existence. I must keep driving. I try not to think. I try to stay free from feeling. I just want to drive and get there safely. I watch the odometer. I keep guessing how much farther I have to go. I sing songs. "When you walk through a storm keep you head up high and don't be afraid of the dark." I cry. I try to think of a happy children's song. I draw a blank. Randy liked that song and asks me to sing it again. I do. I drive on. As I approach Exit 21 on the Thruway, I know I am almost there. We will make it! Only fifteen more minutes.

I drive on. I sing for Randy. I round the bend into Woodbury. I turn the corner onto Ohio Road. There is the house. Mom rushes out. We hug. I did it! I left "Him!" We are helped out of the car and into the house. It feels free in Woodbury.

The kids are glad to be here. Ramona is hungry. I nurse her and relax a little with her in my arms. Four hours of driving and she did not utter a sound. I made it and I am okay. Somehow, I know I can make it now.

Write a chronology of cruelties. How can I do that? I cannot indulge myself and expose my family to the horrors from which I have just emerged. I want to get on with the business of living, but the lawyer insists. He must have a list of cruelties on which to build a case. It has been three months of living apart. He has given me almost no money to support myself or the kids. I am living with my parents in North Bergen. It has been a difficult time. My feelings are quite tender. I am easily swayed by others. I am often not in touch with my feelings. I only know that I can never again be "His" target. Never again can I allow "Him" to spew his wrath upon me. Never again will I permit his diabolique to destroy my sense of self, my feelings, and my critical judgment.

Living in my parents' home has not been without problems. It has also given me a special joy and fulfillment. My children are getting to know their grandparents. So am I. I have not really lived at home since I left for college almost sixteen years ago. That is half my lifetime. I never got to know my parents as an adult. I am getting to know them now. I am fortunate that they have the space, the finances, and the will to help sustain us all since I left.

But my lawyer wants a chronology now, and I can't seem to get off the first page. We got married. We had lived together for six months before our marriage. I knew he was rigid. I knew he was demanding and somewhat unyielding, but I thought he was also capable of love and caring. I believed in what he told me. I believed in his intentions which spoke of love and commitment, although his behavior said hate. His diabolique! I felt it for ten years. I cursed it for ten years. I questioned it for ten years. Yet I never failed to believe in it. He says he loves me, therefore he does. He has sent no money and speaks cruel words to me. I am certain he does not mean his hateful words. I feel that if I explain to him how awful his words are, and how confusing it is to say something one day and deny saying it the next, that he will promise never to do that again. I feel it, yet I know I am wrong. I know that I have explained it hundreds of times. I know he has apologized for his humiliations countless times. He has sworn his love and promised to end the contradictions between his words and his deeds. I thought he had integrity. I have learned he has none.

I do not want to spend any more time dredging up the past. I want to start to live. But he won't send money. I have three children, one an infant. So I have to fight. Here I sit, reflecting on my past. Ten years. A chronology.

ACKNOWLEDGEMENT

Thank you so much to our wonderful editor, Dana Bliss. We could not have done it without you. TK & DP

INTRODUCTION

This book is about litigating child custody and divorce in the context of domestic violence; however, we are going to use the term "domestic abuse" because often there is emotional abuse and no physical violence, but the emotional effects are the same.

Domestic abuse is subtle, harsh, controlling, raw, selfish, emotional, and a host of other similar terms. In short, it is volatile and often physically violent. Attorneys who litigate domestic abuse cases must follow many rules: rules of court, rules of evidence, and rules of civil and criminal procedure—but more—they must be attuned to and be able to follow themes. To accurately see a particular domestic abuse case is to understand its discordant themes. These discordant themes are the "rules" of the abusive relationship. The job of the attorney, judges, and mental health professionals, and even the victims, is to accurately identify these themes. Only then can they be dealt with from both an effective legal and therapeutic perspective.

This book is not anti-male. It is anti-abuse. It is not pro-female. It is pro-family and particularly pro-children. It tries to give the reader an accurate description of how domestic abuse cases are really handled and mishandled by family courts, and how mental health professionals and attorneys can strive to better assist their clients and their clients' children.

A note about language. Classically, most—but not all—victims of domestic abuse are wives or girlfriends (Vagianos, 2015). Victims can of course exist in same gender relationships; they can be men, transgender, etc. For ease of writing and because most victims are women this book identifies the victim of abuse as "she," the "wife," or other similar terms.

The reader will note two typefaces. The first is plain type. This typeface is used to present our professional observations and perspectives. The second is *italic. It is used to convey a storyline.* We hope this interplay of professional information and storyline will be effective and engaging. When the word "I" is used in *italics* in several chapters the chapter is relating a true story.

Some of chapters of this book were previously published. All of them have undergone revisions for purposes of this book.

Finally, there are several chapters that may appear to be primarily written for lawyers. It is done that way for several reasons, despite the fact that the book is intended for mental health professionals. A majority of women who raise the issue of child abuse during the pendency of a divorce lose custody of their child to the named perpetrator (Saunders, 2011). While lawyers need to learn many lessons from that, it is the authors' experience that most lawyers do not really care to learn the specifics relating to dealing with a custody case that involves domestic violence, as it is a small part of their practice.

Even when this is a primary area of an attorney's work, there are factors that mitigate zealous representation in a contested custody case that are not present in other cases. Therefore the mental health professional may find it essential to have an understanding of the process of the legal system in divorce and custody to help assist his or her clients and the attorney representing them. In criminal cases, the lawyer is expected to do everything within ethics and the law to make the government prove its case. He is not asked to be "reasonable" and judges do not generally hold him to account for being zealous.

On the other hand, in family matters both attorneys are frequently called upon by the court to be "reasonable." They often present an outwardly strong position but are strongly encouraged to settle within a range of what the judge thinks is reasonable. The lawyers that use strong tactics become known to the courts and that may affect their effectiveness in other courts in the future. There is a saying among lawyers that the client they are representing will one day be gone but the judge will still be there. They seem to feel they must set aside zealous representation. Mental health professionals that are knowledgeable about how the courts work can assist their clients to set appropriate standards of representation for their lawyers and also assist in selecting new or changing lawyers where necessary.

Matrimonial cases, especially cases involving abuse and/or abused children take place in what may appear to be a lawless or reckless environment because judges do not always strictly adhere to court rules, purportedly in the interest of justice. Attorneys may even be punished with threats of contempt and other sanctions for objecting to "off the record" meetings in judges' chambers, and they may fear that actual zealous representation could hurt, compromise, or dilute their effectiveness in future cases. Mental health professionals who know the client can assure the lawyer of what is required for their client and can assist the client in dealing with the attorney. Both affect the outcomes of cases.

Most lawyers are trained to simply be reactive rather than proactive. They must be cognizant of cost to the client. Too often this approach will hurt the client. A mental health professional who understands the problems inherent in the family court can help the client be assertive with their attorney and can help them create appropriate strategies, including giving direction and instruction to their attorney, such as having all conferences on the record.

Many social workers work within the court system and can benefit from understanding the perspective explained in the book. Mental health professional working outside the court system can assist their clients, understand a sense of urgency in certain circumstances, and be patient with others. All these professionals can benefit when working with battered women and children if they know and understand the system from the outside and the problems that often happen on the inside and within the system.

Mental health professionals working outside the court system can assist their clients understand a sense of urgency in certain circumstances and to be patient in others. They can only do this if they see how the system works and how it gets tainted and understand how to navigate these sometimes treacherous waters.

Ms. Kleinman's mantra to her clients has always been to "take the power you have and use it effectively." Mental health professionals are best at assisting clients to do just that. They can work with their clients and assist to undo the powerlessness and helplessness that is a hallmark of having been battered. They A mentl health professional can then work to figure out strategies with the client if the professional understands how to do so. This book will help.

In child custody cases, the urgency of child protection must trump procrastination. Yet "hurry up and wait" is what happens in court. What a parent believes is a child safety issue may be put off for months, and in other cases requests for relief may be heard without a second party present and it may take months after court action for the other parent to have a day in court. Knowledgeable mental health professionals are often treating victims and understand what their clients are going through. This book will help them navigate through that journey and may help them assist the lawyers. The legal road is not a straight one. It can take many unpredictable curves along the way. Therefore this book is written in such a way that regardless of what an adversary may file in court, the mental health professional can keep perspective with the client and help the client understand the process of going to court.

Indeed, it is also important that mental health professionals and their clients know what a lawyer should be doing and thinking about and how the process should be done. In this way, mental health experts involved with courts can better partner with lawyers, better advocate for their clients, and appropriately critique lawyers.

Sometimes strategies are suggested. This may seem strange to a mental health person. But in order to better assist one's clients it is important to have some ideas for how to create strategies for protection in the court and how some strategies may be viewed by the court. Family court decisions are made by a judge, not a jury. The judge may be cynical or biased. The mental health professional can help by helping their clients view positions from the eyes of a court. In this way the clients will be better served.

DOMESTIC ABUSE, CHILD CUSTODY, AND VISITATION

[1]

A GREAT JUDICIAL FALLACY

Children who have witnessed violence in the home against a parent, or have lived in homes where violence existed, suffer deep and long-lasting emotional effects, even when they are not themselves the victims of violence by the abusive parent (Goddard & Beddi, 2010). Many states have incorporated that knowledge into legislation designed to protect victims of domestic abuse. Thus, by the time a case comes to court on the issue of custody/visitation, the children have already suffered. That being the case, what do we do so they heal and do not suffer any more? Most judges assume that as long as the parents are kept apart, the children will not witness violence and, of course, will not suffer any more. This will serve the children's best interests.

This is the great judicial fallacy.

Too frequently judges end up ignoring all that actually goes into the doctrine of "best interest of the child" and instead they insert the doctrine of "fairness to the parent," often to a violent parent and to the detriment of children. Somehow, regardless of the laws in place, the implementation of these laws is thrown away with findings that place children with the abuser and could never actually be construed as being in the best interest of children. Courts do this as they also ignore the potential need to protect children from abuse. They may use junk science and myths to promote their findings and undermine potential appeals. Moreover, even with the best mental health experts involved, and properly pleaded abuse complaints, the facts of abuse are rarely addressed in many contested cases.

The United States Constitution grants mothers and fathers the right to parent their children (*Parham v. J.R.*, 442 U.S. 584, 1979). The states, too, are charged with protecting children. All states have laws requiring them to intercede to protect children from abuse and neglect even when that protection seemingly requires the state to interfere with the constitutionally guaranteed right to parent.

In family court, when judges are called upon to make custody and visitation decisions, the basis upon which the courts rule is referred to as the "best interest of the child" standard. The state court judge must consider each parent's rights and determine the custodial arrangement that is in that child's best interest. All of the constitutionally protected rights of individuals are assumed to be in place, such as due process and the right to be heard. However, family courts frequently find ways to circumvent these requirements under the guise of best interests, interim orders, and/or emergent circumstances. Indeed many states' court rules permit relaxation of the rules in family court to ensure justice. See, for example, NJ Rule of Court 1:1–2, where unless something is specifically prohibited "any rule may be relaxed or dispensed with by the court in which the action is pending if adherence to it would result in an injustice."

Sadly, too often the result is a combination of factors that largely encompass the judge's level of understanding of domestic violence, child abuse, and inclinations based upon his or her personally held myths, training, and experience. In many cases, judges will resolve the trial between litigating parents without real knowledge and based on their instinct of what is "in the child's best interests," and they become masterful at doing so without stating an appealable foundation by using their discretion as to credibility. It is unusual for an appellate court to overturn a judge who has made credibility decisions on witnesses. Thus trial court is critical. Properly presenting a clients' circumstance is critical.

When a case is litigated through the courts, experts are usually used to assist judges in making the best-interest determination. Judges will appoint mental health professionals for advice in determining best interest. All parents have the constitutional right to put their position forth to the court, stating why the children's best interest is to be in their custody. In doing so, each litigant should have the right to choose an expert. However, state law varies in that some states do not permit a party to engage an expert to evaluate the other party without a court-appointed evaluation first or with the permission from the court. Eventually, all experts should be able to testify as to what custodial arrangement would meet the child's best interest. After listening to direct testimony and cross examination of the parties and experts, only then should a judge make a final decision.

This is the context in which judges, attorneys, and mental health professionals function in the matrimonial milieu. It sounds easy and simple. Almost all matrimonial cases settle without the need for a judge to adjudicate custody or visitation. However, judges are frequently called upon to make "interim" custodial and visitation decisions pending a divorce. The interim decision may be based upon emergent applications with or without conflicting certifications, affidavits, and declarations and before experts are involved, and it may irrevocably limit child contact with the primary caregiver or psychological parent. These interim decisions are critical, as they have lasting effects on the children, and "interim" in a litigated custody case may mean several years and may place children at risk.

Most difficulties arise when there has been spousal abuse or an allegation of spousal or child abuse. Where spousal abuse exists, the interim decision may set the stage for an abusive parent to use the court system to continue to abuse his spouse. A judge's early ruling as to visitation where abuse is alleged is the first message to the child that the court system will or will not help protect him or her from the violent parent, whether the child is a direct victim or not.

Thus, it is at this stage that the court should be most careful to apply what is known about the effects of domestic abuse on children. Yet it is here that this crucial information is often lost or given short shrift. Everyone who works in the field of family violence knows that violence in the home is a continuum of power and control (Walker, 2000). The abuser controls the victim by exerting power, coercion, exploitation, put-downs, threats, and/or physical violence. The level of violence increases as the abuser's need to control escalates. That means that when the batterer has cues that the victim is behaving independently of his control or may be coming out of his control, he exerts a higher level of intimidation, threat, or force. This is a deliberate, controlled pattern of behavior and not passion of a moment (Bancroft, 2015). Nevertheless, this information is rarely integrated by judges as they enter custody/visitation orders, even where restraining orders are in place. Sometimes this is due to flaws in the court's assessment or an imbalance in power between the parties. Too often it is because of poor expert evaluations that do not adequately understand the power and control dynamic in the individual circumstance. It may be the result of a court misapplying a parent's (even an abusive parent's) constitutional right to parent, or in avoidance of a reversal on constitutional grounds.

What does the child's best interest require? Both parents have an equally protected right to parent the child. It is assumed that children need two parents. In theory, the law should attempt to integrate what is known about the effects of domestic abuse, as it grants wide latitude to judges about appropriate custody and visitation orders. Our criticism with judges comes first during the initial phase of divorce/custody litigation in the failure to apply the best interest standard to the law as it incorporates what is known about domestic abuse and to err if at all on the side of the physical and emotional well-being of the child. Instead, courts apply their own "assumptions" about custody and about violence and keeping parties separate.

The operable words of error are the fact that the parents are not together "any more." Too many judges believe that it is appropriate, if not correct, to provide the violent parent access to the child where there is no substantiated child abuse apart from the spousal abuse, despite the fact that the children are harmed by violence to their other parent as a result of that abuse. By way of example, ". . . the Legislature found and declared that domestic violence is a serious crime against society. It found that thousands of persons in this State were regularly beaten, tortured and in some cases killed by their spouses or cohabitants. That a significant number of women were assaulted while pregnant. That victims of domestic violence came from all social and economic backgrounds. That there is a positive correlation between spousal abuse and child abuse and that children, even if they are not themselves physically assaulted, suffer deep and lasting emotional effects from exposure to domestic violence" (The Prevention of Domestic Violence Act N.J.S.A.2C:25-17).

When the contest is custody during divorce, judges tend to ignore the proper application of domestic abuse knowledge and seem to rely on the assumption that children need two parents (and other myths that are not supported in the psychological literature) and their constitutionally protected right to parent. In the process, a child's safety is set aside.

There remains reluctance by the courts to straightforwardly deal with allegations of incest, child sexual abuse, or emotional or physical abuse. In jurisdictions throughout the country, a protective parent who raises these issues in open court is often punished for even raising the issue by loss of custody and/or visitation. In addition to other reasons expressed by the court, the protective parent may be disregarded as "too angry" to have or share custody.

Where there has been abuse in the home, there must be an initial assessment of what the impact already has been on the child in the home, as well as the potential effect on the child if there is contact with the predatory parent. Unless the suffering that has already occurred is recognized and considered by the court at the outset, the child's best interest cannot be met. It follows that the first consideration by the court to meet the child's best interest would be to attempt to heal the suffering the child has been made to endure.

When judges assume that simply keeping the parents apart is enough, the suffering that has already taken place is ignored. This initial judicial fallacy actually neglects the child's needs and gives children the message that they will not be protected from a violent parent. The stage is then set for the violent parent to continue to control the battered spouse through the court system. The non-violent, protective parent is forced to battle for custody to attempt to protect her child from harm, which often puts her in the light of seeming angry and vengeful rather than protective—a parental catch-22. Thus, in litigating at this critical stage, the history of the suffering of the child should not be ignored by counsel (or the litigant), and that information should be placed unapologetically and directly before the court if child protection is a serious goal of the advocate and representative.

The attorney representing the victim is in a difficult circumstance. How does one combat the great judicial fallacy? Why do attorneys feel as if they are doing something wrong to assert to the court that children need a time to heal without contact with the predatory parent? The answer: they believe judges will dismiss that argument out of hand. Even the attorneys that agree to raise this issue, when on the record in open court, often get called back to a judge's chambers, where they sometimes undermine the safety of the child and the stated goals of their client by diluting their position and even telling judges that they "have to raise this because of client insistence" or some other weak apology statement.

What can be done? After all, the right to parent is constitutionally protected. In the best of family circumstances, a child is better with two parents. The parents are each legally entitled to parent. Courts should not ignore situations, however, where the right to parent collides with the child's need for safety. If the judge, at the interim ruling on custody/visitation, applies the findings of the professional literature, there would be no collision between the law and its application. And ultimately the child might have a viable relationship even with an abusive parent.

This book is not designed to pontificate. While there is frustration evident in our writing, we are acutely aware that there is a way to function within the system to force the system to look at the law and more properly apply it to children. This book will advocate certain guiding principles that shine a light on achieving child protection even within this flawed system.

Litigation is time-consuming and expensive. We hope this book advocates for children sufficiently so that mental health and legal professionals, including judges, will realize that children will not only be better protected, but will also have a better chance to have a relationship with the predatory spouse if they are given time to heal and are adequately protected. The challenge is to get the judge to understand, at the initial stage of litigation, that the law protecting children actually requires a different assumption be applied. As we explain throughout the book, what too often happens in this stage is ignored by attorneys, and it is not until children are irreparably harmed, or at risk of being irreparably harmed, that a judge is then forced to separate the children from the abusive parent. We have also seen death of children at the failure by the court to take seriously the concerns of a protective parent.

Studies have shown that the effect of even a single incident of violence may have long-term effects on children as victims (Bancroft, 2004). Most domestic abuse laws do not make a distinction between the effects on children of non-physical domestic abuse, such as harassment or stalking, from physical violence. But judges still fall into one component of the great judicial fallacy: If we remove the child from the abusive circumstances and can keep the parents apart, all abuse to the child is over. The family court system, in attempting to protect the constitutional rights of parents, often neglects the needs of their children, and there is no uniform definition of abuse. Why do the courts not automatically insist that children receive appropriate counseling by skilled mental health professionals, trained in the effects of domestic abuse on children? The reason, it appears to us, is that the judges don't believe the children really suffered or continue to suffer. They insert their own values and beliefs instead of suspending them, as they are supposed to do. They believe in the great judicial fallacy.

They believe this serves the entirety of the child's best interests. Each time they enter an order based upon it, they potentially create further suffering for children and make the problem even more difficult to rectify.

This is the position that every judge is placed in when a visitation order is issued, before those children have healed from the suffering of being a witness to their mother being abused—even absent abuse directly to the child. It is easy to contemplate such fear and the need for healing from a trauma when we speak about violence by strangers. Now imagine you watched your father hit your mother and heard her cry out in pain or out of fear. Your reaction would be the same. When will he do this to me? What do I have to do to keep myself safe? What did my mother do wrong so that he hurts her like that? Too often the courts ignore these images and ignore the suffering of these child witnesses.

Children quite naturally love both of their parents. But in promoting a child's best interests, sometimes one needs to first take a simple look at the circumstances. Once children have seen someone they love hurt by someone else they love, they know that the batterer is capable of hurting and that it is possible for them to be hurt by that person also, even in the name of love. If a child has already been hurt directly by that parent, a special abuse court should hear that issue separately and apart from issues of custody, and the non-hurting parent should not be required to prosecute that claim as if it were a claim for custody—it is instead a claim for child protection.

A spousal abuser doesn't proclaim hate for the abused spouse. He proclaims his love. Thus a child sees a violent definition of the word love. He thinks, "If my father loves my mother and hurts her, then he can love me and hurt me, too." How much simpler can it be? The helpless child in that circumstance has no protector. The only thing is for the child to accommodate and try to avoid getting injured.

In domestic abuse cases, less is often more. In other words, removing a violent parent from a child's life for a period of time, to give treatment to the child, let the child heal, and restore confidence in the non-violent parent's ability to properly protect the child, gives that child an opportunity to experience a safe relationship with the violent spouse. But if such children are not protected, they may never learn to trust that anyone can protect them, and what's worse, surely their best interests have not been safeguarded by the court.

An attorney once sardonically explained how the courts make their determinations on visitation issues. Quite frankly, he said, the court assumes everyone is lying and they try to figure out what is best despite the lies.

What bothers us is that when the victims finally leave their abusers, they are often maligned by their attorneys and the courts for trying to protect their children from the batterer even though the suspension of contact may be an important part of treatment for children who have witnessed violence. Judges, supposedly adequately trained in domestic abuse, somehow take that knowledge and discard it when applying best interest to domestic abuse circumstances. They blame the victim of spouse abuse and accuse her of wanting to withhold the child from the other parent. Too often junk science is applied (see Chapter 11, Family Courts Must Demand Science). They cannot, or do not, understand that a woman's incredible passion to keep her children safe from their violent father is healthy and protective and not an attempt to alienate. If a separate court was handling the matter and it was not a contest between two parents about the divorce itself, it might be easier for a judge to understand and apply knowledge about intimate violence.

Presently, in the divorce arena, it makes even less sense to judges that a woman fights visitation when, as a wife, she lived with the abuser for a long time with the child. Experience has taught us that frequently women assume courts will protect them and the children, where they themselves may have been unable to do so.

It is almost as if the judges say to themselves, "you didn't think it was bad enough that your child needed protection then," "you chose this guy," "you had a child," or "you suddenly decide the guy's no good as a parent, when you are good and ready to leave—why now?"

Essentially, the judges assume it couldn't have really been that bad or the woman would not have stayed. They find her vindictive or angry or hysterical. They enter visitation orders and ignore the impact. In short, they focus on the woman rather than the needs of the child. There is an abundance of literature on why women stay in abusive relationships (Halket et al., 2014). Instead of looking at the reality of why women appear frantic or upset or overly cautious, too many judges assume the victim is at least partially to blame. They see her current behavior as hysterical or frantic and attribute that as a cause of the child's state of mind.

A twist of logic has occurred. Women repeatedly complain to judges as they witness the fear of their children. The children believe their mothers did not adequately protect them. They become angry and try to accommodate to their father to protect themselves. They know the violence of which their father is capable. The courts do not see the need to protect and instead deny the mother's requests to protect. The judge then begins to see the protective parent as the real cause of the problem. This is another critical juncture. The more frequently a woman returns to court to seek help, the more she appears unreasonable and interfering with the fostering of love and affection between the child and the other parent. Even mental health professionals start to see the mother as the "uncooperative" parent, foiling the professionals' attempts to diffuse the situation. At times, some are trying to do the judge's job (making custody or visitation decisions without taking the court's time), or maybe trying to re-unify the broken family or input other personal values or goals. Strategically it also opens the door for the abusive parent to raise issues about the other parent and seek more contact or take away all contact from the protective parent. Too often they win. Judges tend to judge these mothers harshly.

Sometimes, the women themselves do not understand the impact of the violence on the children. They agree to visitation. They dutifully support the rights of the father to see his children. Still, that doesn't change the child's fear. Even when the victim agrees to visitation, problems may display themselves later in a child.

If the child's fear is initially neglected, it does not go away. When the victim does attempt to bring the problems to the attention of the court, the court no longer looks at the domestic abuse aspect. Instead, the child's problems are assumed to be jointly caused, or caused by the parent who is living with the child. When that happens, the court is blaming the victim. The victim becomes even more powerless, as the batterer seizes upon the logic the courts use in assuming that the mother, the residential custodian, is at least equally to blame for problems in the relationship between the father and the child, and the batterer accuses the woman of brainwashing and the road is paved for the mother to lose custody.

Inadvertently, courts allow litigation to become full blown instead of seeing the initial flaw in their own orders in the great judicial fallacy. The judges have actually helped teach the children the lesson that their mother is unable to provide adequate protection. The violent spouse gets the court to do his bidding. The victim must go on the defensive and must attempt to prove the damage in the father/child relationship is not her fault. If only the court had recognized the child's need to heal from the beginning, the litigation could not have proceeded in this way. The mode has now changed to "kill the messenger." The mother/victim is not seen as protective but is seen as the cause, and custody becomes a serious issue in the eyes of the judge. In fact, it then becomes a question of how a protective parent can maintain custody of the children she is raising. This is how abusers get judges to hurt their wives the most. The initial needs of the child were overlooked. When the victim does assert a problem, the failure to have recognized it when visitation was first addressed is seen as a reason to either disbelieve it or assume there is another cause. It is at this time that a detailed complaint for divorce that outlines the history and the particular dynamics of the control by the abuser is essential to bring forth to the court's attention.

In our experience too few judges actively protect children. They may learn the statistics and they may learn the problems with victims. The problem is that once they are on the bench, judges don't seem to actually differentiate between an "ordinary" custody case and a custody case where there is a history of domestic abuse. Most cases settle amicably. But in the latter circumstance there is an essential ingredient that requires a different application. The parents rarely come into the family court having equal financial resources, competent emotionality for litigation, and with the child's safety as a primary goal. There is always a "tilt" for all of the reasons we shall describe. It is hoped that the complaint for divorce has outlined in detail why the victim and child need the court's protection and why and how this is not a typical divorce.

When the custody issue arises later in a case and the judge has had an opportunity to observe the parents, the court must suspend personal judgments about human nature. Domestic abuse happens in private. The impact of domestic abuse cannot be derived from hasty observations of a parent in court. There is no psychological profile of the batterer, so the judge has no particular characteristics to look for. There is no socio-economic group that is immune from domestic abuse. Thus, we are asking judges to suspend whatever notions they might have about people and insert professional mental health knowledge about domestic abuse. It usually does not work.

For example, imagine the violent parent as a middle-class or professional man. He is well-dressed and polite. He is soft-spoken to the court and in the court. He has been financially responsible and works and earns an above-average salary. He may even be a superior employee or employer. He may be handsome and charming and have a new girlfriend with him who appears unafraid and is a good person, willing to swear the defendant has never abused her. These are all qualities upon which we are taught to judge others. It is contrary to our belief system to picture this individual as violent in his own home. It is even more unimaginable to assume this man has caused harm to his child. Such men appear calm. They appear appropriately outraged at the attack upon their integrity or upon their ability to parent.

At these times, it is most important for the court to remember the impact of domestic abuse on children in the long term. Instead, most judges discard that and fall into the trap of blaming the victim or believing she is lying or exaggerating. Sometimes the women claim that their young children come home from visitation angry and upset—sometimes even acting out violently against them. They report this. Judges see this as symptomatic of a mother's inability to control a young child, rather than examining the cause of it as reactive to the other parent and feeling safe in the home of the mother.

This will happen until we combat the great judicial fallacy and are willing to take a stand at the outset that contact with the batterer is inconsistent with the child's best interest until the child is sufficiently healed. All cases raising domestic violence and child abuse require recognition that the matter is different from a generalized understanding of traditional divorces. How can this be accomplished?

[2]

DEFINING THE PROBLEM

Representing a Battered Woman in Divorce

While modern day society has taken steps in recognizing the plight of battered women, both the court and the legal system have been slow to account for the special needs and circumstances of the battered woman. Specialized knowledge and training is required for attorneys and mental health professionals for this kind of legal representation. The way a case from its inception is presented to court is critical. Without special understanding of the dynamics of domestic abuse it is impossible to properly present the case, thereby handicapping the victim in court. Where there are children, the threat of loss of custody, frequently threatened by the father even before the pendency of a divorce, often keeps the victim compliant even during the pendency of litigation.

The family court has broad discretionary power. At the initial phases of a divorce case important decisions by a family court judge are made on the basis of affidavits, certifications, and even hearsay evidence. These early decisions may affect the final outcome of child support, alimony, equitable distribution, community property, and custody/visitation awards. Accordingly, early information may have long-term effects.

Context is critical for everything in a family court. Taking a family history cannot be minimized. Attorneys and mental health professionals must always ask a client to describe the first real argument she had with her spouse before she was married. We find that much does not change from that first argument to the "final straw." The problem is that specifics are critical because battered women invariably minimize and, as a result, are not terribly good reporters of history. Thus, mental health professionals who do therapy for women and do evaluations for the court or lawyers must ask some probing historical questions and recognize that the process is not necessarily linear for women who are emotionally or physically battered. One question to ask is, "How did you resolve your first real dispute with your husband, even before you were married?" We find that the relationship mechanisms existing long before marriage continue to exist well into the marriage.

Our experience has been that many women who end up being battered seek to please before marriage. They set their own needs aside. They capitulate and absorb. It begins with empathy for their husbands' feelings and becomes a pattern of setting their own needs and feelings aside. This pattern gets exploited by their emotionally battering partner and never seems to change.

We have found that the women at the time of marriage are actually more stable, healthier, and more capable of flexibility and therefore probably start out more emotionally healthy than their husbands, not realizing the emotional impact to them over time. The flexible strong woman begins to lose her center, but there is no one defining moment until, for almost an inexplicable reason, she leaves.

Anecdotally, it seems that batterers choose strong women who, over the course of the emotionally battering relationship, become insecure and dependent. Mental health professionals can help courts understand that these men are rigid and unyielding and less emotionally healthy, and they can show how and why it may look otherwise. When most of these women enter the legal world, there is a naïveté, an expectation that her lawyer will understand and the court will fix things. Her stance is usually filled with conclusions rather than with the substance of what happened and how she may have contributed, albeit unwittingly, to let it occur.

Untrained lawyers, mental health professionals, and courts do not understand that abusers tend to be masters of deflection, and they put on to others what is actually true of themselves; they spin things, claiming their wives are the cause of the problems. Emotional abuse can cause a learned helplessness as women, through years of struggle, have tried to adapt and accommodate to their husbands' often escalating demands. By the time they leave many women have become convinced of how harmful their spouses are to them and to their children, and there is an unrealistic expectation that others will instantly understand. When others don't "get it," the women may appear unstable, and thus their husbands' statements about their instability look real to the untrained observer—the court.

For all of these reasons and others, it is critical for abused women to first have help in unraveling their history—from how they started in a relationship to where they ended up. What were the woman's expectations for a marriage when they were young? How did they get so far away from that? The women's valiant efforts at dispute mediation in the marriage, often resolved by her capitulation, are often at the heart of this. Good mental health professionals can teach lawyers how to unravel the history and show how the husband has deflected blame. They can help show that her attempts to appease the batterer's unending insecurity and self-centeredness contributed to her appearing unraveled. Mental health professionals need to probe to try to figure out how it began so they can explain the mechanisms they see operating.

Most often, complaints for divorce provide the minimum amount of information necessary to finalize an actual divorce. For the battered woman, that is not enough. Complaints for divorce do not tell the relevant and critical story. If there are concerns about child custody or visitation and/or emotional or physical abuse, or all of these, as an integral part of the breakdown of the family, then describing the history of the relationship in a complaint for divorce is necessary to set the stage for the entire case. This avoids the later question: If there was abuse why didn't she tell us earlier? It also helps to unravel an abuser's deflection of blame.

In addition, where there is abuse in a marriage, it is often accompanied by behavior about which the battered spouse is ashamed and which her spouse has threatened to reveal to others. It is disclosure of her own behavior that she often fears most. She may feel responsible for her own battering as though she could have prevented it, if only she behaved differently or did not provoke it in some way. Those feelings may inhibit her from disclosing violence even to her attorney until she is later confronted with allegations against her by her spouse or unless her attorney asks for it.

The attorney must ask for and elicit from the victim information about herself that she fears the batterer or the court may use to take the children away. For example, a victim may have used alcohol or drugs. She herself may have used severe corporal punishment on her children, though she expresses that she is opposed to its use. The attorney must ask if her husband has in any way ever threatened to use this information against her. Victims believe their spouses will win. They often feel defeated at the outset.

In general, during the course of a case there will be information that a victim wants to withhold from her attorney and the court. However, it is often the information the victim most desires to withhold about herself during the pendency of a case and about which she is most ashamed that may be the same behavior her spouse has threatened to disclose to others about her. For example, a cocaine user, a mother of two young children, came for representation after she lost custody of her children. Her spouse had disclosed her drug use to the court during the course of litigation. The mother lost custody despite the husband's history of serious spousal abuse, some of which the children had witnessed. At the outset of new legal representation after the loss of custody, she sought to renew the case. She was strongly urged to acknowledge her prior drug problem and enter a drug rehab clinic. She listened to the advice and regained custody of her children shortly after her release from the clinic. It was only through her participation in a treatment center as an inpatient that the court became convinced that the children were safe in her care. Her honesty about her own problem caused the court to find her credible later.

Attorneys should encourage the disclosure of crucial information before a victim is confronted with allegations by her abuser. She then has the opportunity to be candid while also explaining the surrounding circumstances without being defensive. When clients disclose information initially and do not wait until their spouse discloses it in an effort to gain custody, the client is less likely to lose custody, even temporarily.

During an abusive relationship a woman may behave negatively to her children. When the abuse stops, her negative behavior may stop. Sometimes women drink to excess or take illegal drugs. These behaviors may be a reaction to the abuse and may easily cease or diminish once the abuser leaves the home. We have heard from many women who have suffered from these and other problems, and have been in psychotherapy during the marriage, that the battering was never even disclosed in therapy. Remarkably, they themselves saw no causal relationship at the time. They merely felt desperate. Thus, it is critical that a context from which the entire case can be viewed is understood by the attorney and then set up for a court at the outset.

By failing to address domestic abuse and its impact, a case becomes ripe for an abusive spouse to take custody of the children. While most divorce cases are resolved amicably between the parties with the help of counsel, a small fraction goes to trial. In those that do go to trial, custody is usually won by the father.

Where the abuse is not disclosed until custody is an actual issue before the court to resolve, or where the wife fails to disclose any of her own negative behavior, the plausibility of her story is easily attacked by an adversary. Credibility is essential to prevailing on any issue in court. Determination of credibility is at the discretion of a trial court and is difficult to overturn on appeal. Where someone has not been forthright about his or her own issues, the adversary's attack may then be more easily believed by the court. This actually sets the stage for a loss of custody from the non-violent spouse and feeds right into the threats of the batterer to expose her weaknesses to the court and thereby take custody of the children.

Practitioners in the field of family law are often cynical about women's reactions to their abusers, especially when there has been no physical violence or bruises. They ask themselves, for example, how can she say that she is afraid of her husband when last night she shared a bed? An attorney must understand that emotionally battered women are vulnerable to coercion. If the attorney does not understand, the attorney may incorrectly assume since the battered woman was never physically harmed she has no basis for fear or that her telling of her coercion is a mere manipulation.

Sadly, lawyers and family court judges still distinguish between the effects of violence on victims of "hard core" violence from the impact of minor physical violence or psychological abuse, which often lies below the surface and is not as clearly evident. Unfortunately, this mistaken distinction persists despite the fact that mental health professionals who have defined domestic abuse and who work with victims of domestic abuse recognize that the psychological impact of physical versus emotional abuse is similar (Eisikovits & Band-Winterstein, 2014).

The distinction made by judges between the effects of physical and emotional abuse must be recognized and taken into account by an attorney who prepares a case. Also, an attorney must be able to argue to the court, based on the specific facts of each individual case, that the distinctions between emotional and physical violence are incorrect and all judgments that flow from those misperceptions or false assumptions are in error. The need for domestic abuse laws is predicated on the need to protect victims, prevent domestic abuse, and minimize the effects of family violence on women and children. For instance, the New Jersey Prevention of Domestic Violence Act recognizes harassment and other non-physically violent acts as a part of domestic abuse. But if the basis for the law that includes non-violent forms of domestic abuse is not properly understood by those who advocate for victims, the victims are effectively without an advocate in court. Further, if a problem arises about visitation issues during the pendency of divorce, and no basis for concern for the victim or her children has previously been expressed to the court, the woman may appear to be manipulative or unreasonable instead of appropriately concerned.

A case where physical violence is well-documented and a case where there is no prior history require similar preparation, knowledge, and understanding. An attorney preparing a case involving psychological abuse must prepare it no differently than a case where physical violence is present. Trained mental health professionals can assist lawyers in understanding this. The impact of the use of threats or coercion on a victim or her children cannot be considered by the court where an attorney has not previously raised it as an issue. If the attorney does not understand it as domestic abuse, that victim is at a legal disadvantage. What is worse, however, is that if the children become at risk, or later physical violence is threatened or occurs, the violence may be viewed by the court as being a single incident of aberrant behavior, out of character of the defendant caused by stress of divorce, rather than a continuation of a pattern of domestic abuse. Domestic abuse experts recognize that abusers seek to control. We have found that violence escalates to the level necessary to exact a desired amount of control over the victim. Domestic abuse often begins with threats or harassment. If the threat is not enough to control the victim, the batterer escalates to a level necessary to gain compliance to his demands. The abuser often uses the court system to perpetuate his control. Many married victims are not on par financially with their husbands. The abuser exerts power by failing to provide support or other necessary finances. Legal fees may be costly. The fact is that the court system can and is used by the abuser to exert control and thus cause additional stress to a victim. This must be mitigated by judges to keep the litigants on an even financial playing field.

Long after a legal relationship has ended a victim still understands the special language her abuser uses to threaten her or her children, though his threat may seem innocuous to others. Lawyers and judges must begin to accept that victims usually underreport violence.

Not all battered women have restraining orders, and incidents of violence may never have been brought to the attention of police or the courts before a divorce action begins. In fact, physical violence sometimes begins after divorce proceedings commence as batterers then act out against children as a means of controlling their spouse or forcing the spouse to return. Sometimes women fear getting a restraining order as they feel they can better protect themselves without it.

I recall a case many years ago in which a woman had suffered severe physical abuse during a marriage but never sought an order of protection. On the heels of a trial she spoke to her husband and believed he would be violent to her. It was only then that she sought an order of protection. There was no specific threat to hurt her or her child. She viscerally felt a threat by the tone in his voice, a tone he used before each prior beating. She sought and obtained a restraining order.

Women are at risk of extreme violence after leaving a violent relationship. When victims stand up for themselves, their abusers may become enraged and violence may escalate. The courts must be sensitized to the subtle and continuing implication of a history of a relationship where coercion is exerted and intimidation and/or physical violence is used as a device to control another individual.

There are numerous inconsistencies still permitted in the law. For example, some states do not require victims of domestic abuse to go to court-ordered mediation of visitation issues. It is understood that a victim cannot have an arms-length relationship with her abuser. However, judges regularly enter orders requiring victims to negotiate visitation with their abuser. In the public arena no one would think to require contact between a victim and her assailant, much less negotiate a centrally important issue. Why then, when we know the spouse is a victim, do judges require such contact?

Too often, once a divorce action begins, the violence is easily dismissed by the attorney as insignificant or unimportant to the issues before the court. It may also be dismissed because an attorney believes including that information may be inconsistent with seeking mutual consent to all issues.

Judges may disbelieve the victim and may accuse her of wanting an advantage in a custody action and seeking to get a legal advantage. When only lip service is given to the victim, even though the law may require a legal presumption in her favor where violence is admitted or found to be present by a court, children may wind up more at risk of becoming pawns in a custody struggle.

The law encourages strong parental relationships. Women are told by counsel that they must prepare their children for liberal visitation. However, if the attorney does not realize the critical nature of dealing with the family dynamics of abuse, as distinct from a non-violent relationship, and fails to alert the court to the child as a victim witness of battering, or assumes a child is no longer intimidated by the violent parent because the actual violence has ended, the victim or her children may continue to be victims.

Domestic abuse victims often consider their abusers to be good fathers. The attorney must explain the correlation between spousal abuse and child abuse in general and explain how it applies in the particular case. Domestic abuse is a control mechanism of the abuser's spouse and children. We have heard countless iterations that violence in the home is a loss of control. We query rhetorically, "How then does this same individual work in a high-stress job and never lose control?" Sometimes victims agree to arrangements for visitation because they believe their concerns are unimportant or will not be understood, or they go against what they believe is correct to give a judge the impression they are reasonable. Sometimes they believe that everything will get better if they simply go along with what their estranged spouse demands. They have not yet learned that as soon as they do, the spouse will up the ante. These contradictions need to be explored by lawyers and mental health professionals or the children may be at further risk of harm as batterers may use the children to further control their wives.

Often abusers proclaim love for their victim even as they abuse them. This same proclamation is made to their children. The effect of violence on the children is nevertheless profound. Batterers often appear charming, coherent, and stable. They exist in all strata of society. They often boast to their wives that no one will believe there was violence. They may be likeable, their violent tendencies being completely hidden, except to their immediate family. Victims of abuse rely on their attorneys to present their case in the best way it can be presented. Victims may be difficult clients. They make frequent phone calls and ask endless questions. They may appear dependent or angry, or they may fear being a nuisance and not call with important concerns. Their expectations are not always realistic. They may ask for advice, yet make unending challenges to the advice they are given. They are easily intimidated by a strong attorney and may go along with recommendations out of a feeling of pressure rather than true consent.

To be an effective counsel and mental health professional for a battered woman takes time and requires special knowledge. These requirements are not optional, they are essential.

Often the judges will refer to violence as problems between the parties and place no blame. This makes the victim feel as though the judge does not understand and increases her feelings of intimidation by her abuser. Legal representation of a battered woman in divorce is a distinct role in that attorneys must know more than the law. They must have knowledge of the special traits of the victim in order to even elicit from her the information necessary to properly advocate on her behalf. Special knowledge and sensitivity to the dynamics of the victim and the battering cycle is essential. They may even call the court's attention to the use of special language. Only when mental health professionals, attorneys, and judges become more sensitized to these issues will there be hope that victims of domestic abuse will be better protected.

[3]

MEMORY

I managed to write the list of cruelties. I wrote 50 pages. At first I sat down and couldn't write a thing. My mind would go blank. I could not think of anything which would be considered cruel. What had he done that was so awful that the judge would think was cruel? I walked out with three children. I started a fight the day I left. I was the one who left home. He now called each day to say he loved me and the kids. He called each day to say please come back home. "Pocono Vista was never home." "I'm not the same person you left "an hour ago." My head would start repeating one-liners. I could not remember my life. I had been too busy living it, surviving it, to remember. All those panic attacks I had when I thought we would separate. He would hold me in his arms and promise never to leave me.

Why did I ever even have panic attacks? I had never had one before. I was always so strong, tenacious, and fearless. Nothing made sense. What was the matter with me that at the age of 30, I was now living in my parents' home with three children, my dog, and no money of my own?

My parents' home was a home/office. I sat in my father's secretary's office and used her typewriter. I thought of going in to my mother to ask for help. What did he do that was so awful? Why am I here? Maybe I should go back.

"Tell me," my mother said, "What was he like to live with? I remember when David was born we came to your house with a fresh blueberry pie, Sidney's favorite. He threw us out of the house. You let him. Why, Tammy? How did things get so bad that you let your husband throw us out of your home?" I had no answer. Worse. I had no memory.

I had no answer. The thought of no memories terrified me. Why could I not remember? Before I chose to forget it, I needed to recall it. Finally, I simply began to write. We met. I was young. He was a college professor. He was smart and worldly. He seemed revered by everyone I met. His manner was self-effacing. He spoke slowly and softly. He was articulate. He was so sensitive that when he talked about his first marriage, he cried at the loss of his two young children. He gave them up. His wife had an affair and told him they were not his kids. He had raised them and loved them but he gave them up. I saw no paradox. I held him as he cried. I felt touched by his tears. I asked no more.

It is now two years later. We are about to go to trial on the issue of visitation between Sidney and the kids. For two years we have been fighting. I wrote about the cruelties. I told my lawyer how difficult life was. I could never really explain it though. It is only beginning to make sense now. I had fallen head over heels in love, in admiration, in adoration. He knew that. He used that. I never met anyone he worked with. I was never brought to any work-related activities. My family wasn't permitted in our home. It was too disruptive. When I spoke to my mother, Sidney and I always had a fight. He would accuse me of saying things that she wanted me to say, believing what she wanted me to believe. I wasn't allowed to buy anything without permission. I could only buy what he said I needed. I wanted to please him. He was a revered college professor. He was right and I would learn to have good values. I stopped seeing my siblings and my parents to try to prove I was really independent. He valued independence. I went one whole year not talking to them. He said they would never be out of my system. I tried.

It didn't make sense, but I loved him. I wanted him to respect me. He couldn't respect someone who was like a child and so dependent on their parents for emotional support or love.

He taught me how to think. He taught me how to buy clothes. He didn't like me to wear make-up. He did not let me get my nails done or my hair cut. I wore make-up when we met. I had my nails done when we dated. But I was now a married woman. He did not want other men looking at me. I had to keep myself unattractive. Although he said I was more beautiful when I was plain looking.

He would get angry in a quiet way. He would get angry and disdainful. He let me know I was stupid and immature. He'd offer to help me to grow up. He would tell me, in a tone I still can't replicate, that one day I would get it. He hoped. Then we would be happy. I tried to get it. I desperately wanted to please him. I believed if I pleased him, we would be happy. He would then pay me a compliment. He would tell me I was finally independent like he was. He didn't need anyone. He went to work but hated and scoffed at those with whom he worked. He hated his father and barely spoke with his brother. He was independent. He needed no one. But he loved me. I was lucky to have him. He bought us a home. He chose beautiful furniture. He didn't like the furniture I liked and he had a way of making me feel foolish for liking something so awful. I stopped telling him what I liked.

I would ask him first. He came home for lunch every day. I had no time for friends. I got pregnant the first month after we got married. I was only twenty-two. He wanted me to rely on him, not my parents. So I did. He left late for work each day. That was a perk of being a professor. He came home for lunch. Back from work by four. I had no friends. No time for friends. I was thrilled he wanted to spend so much time with me that I lost touch with everyone I knew. I stopped working to ensure our time together. He never told me I had to, but when he had met my friends he thought they were so immature. I dropped them.

Ten years together. He had a heart attack. I went into therapy when I was falling apart at the seams. I had lost touch with any feelings. I believed I did not feel. I had come to believe that my feelings were always wrong, so I needed to change them. I had gone from a happy, rather carefree young woman, to an old woman afraid of her shadow.

The last two years have been rough. I finally borrowed enough money from my family for a lawyer and to get set up in an apartment. I managed to get the bare necessities from Sidney for the kids. Ramona lives in a pantry off the kitchen. I sleep on a mattress on the bare floor. David sleeps on a hide-a-bed. Nothing else fits. My sister gave us an air conditioner. I found a used dishwasher and hooked it up with a friend. I no longer have panic attacks. I was president of the PTO. Ramona is in nursery school and Randy is in kindergarten.

There have been two years of court battles. He wants a lot of time with the kids. I finally left to protect the kids. Randy was stammering. David used to stand motionless, afraid to speak. He would isolate himself in his room for hours on end.

He would cry. When Ramona was born, life became unbearable. Sidney had retired on disability. We moved to an isolated house in the mountains. He was with me all the time. He told me what to do at every moment. He had a temper which seethed. I wasn't allowed to say how I felt. I wasn't allowed to like anything or want anything. Neither could the kids. If he said they liked vanilla, they liked vanilla. We all walked on eggshells around the house. When he would rage, we all knew what we had to do to protect ourselves—and we did it.

He talked to me with contempt. One day David, age 8, talked to me in the same tone. My heart sank. I spent my life for the kids. I didn't work or go to school. My job was Mom. And my job as Mom couldn't tolerate being hated by my children for allowing their father to spew his wrath upon them. They would hate me for allowing it. I couldn't take the pain of even the thought. When I heard David talk to me in that tone, the same tone his father used day after day, hour after hour, I just could not bear it. I heard Randy stammer as he tried to talk to his father. A tiny three year-old, shaking as he spoke. I held my nursing infant and knew I had to get out. I got out. Left, just like that. It probably seemed impulsive. I had thought about it for years. When Ramona was born, I was not going to go back with him. There was no laughter in our home.

Everything was an ordeal. Everything was difficult. The mundane was difficult, the ordinary was difficult. The threat of dying was the same as the joy of living. I finally got the strength to leave.

Then he set out to take them from me. If I couldn't protect them, I should have stayed. Why suffer with virtual poverty to just give them over to him the same as if he were still living with them? I had to fight. I tried to get him to understand, but he would not. I tried to get my lawyer to understand, but he could not. What he finally understood was that I believed I had to protect my children. The trial is scheduled. I am terrified. I am tired. I feel alone. Will I lose the love of my children because I could not protect them? I do not want to take them from him. In fact, I want to give them the tools to deal with him. For that, they need time away from him, not more time with him to be forced into complicity.

How strange it is that the fight to protect them is also a fight to allow them to have a relationship with him so they do not idealize him. He will never believe it. I hope they will one day understand.

The judge has to decide how much time my children spend with him. My ability to give them a safe environment is determined by a strange judge in black robes. I know these two years have caused me to reflect. I still have few memories and flashbacks. I cannot yet really feel. I sometimes cry for no reason, but am unaware of why I am crying.

My life is centered on the need to give my children stability. I will leave the country rather than turn them over and let them be destroyed.

That knowledge has given me peace and also terrifies me. If I leave, I will not be back. My children are just beginning to know they have family, a large family, and accepting family with unconditional love for them. If I leave, they will lose that forever. It is now in the hands of the court.

[4]

LANGUAGE IS IMPORTANT
TO VICTIMS

What a court says to a litigant during litigation has a significant impact on the litigant. The most natural language for a judge to use stems from the Constitution of the United States. However, language that may on its face appear to express equal rights and equal protection under the law may actually be communicating the opposite, setting the stage for the perpetrator of domestic abuse to feel emboldened by the court. Paradoxically, such language creates a sense of disempowerment. Thus, to guarantee equal protection requires a special sensitivity to the impact of language.

The nuances of the words have significant impact on both victims and perpetrators. It is important for the court and others in court to use language that will communicate accurately to both the victim and the perpetrator. To properly understand the impact, it is helpful to have an overview of the setting in which the language is used, as well as the process that takes place. Picture the scenario in which the parties have separated as a result of domestic abuse. The wife has been granted a restraining order where, after an evidentiary hearing, a judge has made a finding that there has been domestic abuse and the husband has been removed from the marital residence. The husband has been the primary financial support for the family. The wife has had the responsibility for the day-to-day care of the children. While she has held a job, she earns less than the husband, and thus is dependent upon the husband for most of the family support. The wife still lives in the marital residence using her salary, as well as the support she gets from her husband, and is responsible to pay bills. Because she earned less than her husband during the marriage, the wife has had virtually all the responsibility to handle children's extracurricular activities, appointments with the doctor and dentist, as well as making social arrangements for the children, transporting the children to and from school, and helping with homework.

Once the parties are in court, there is an expectation that both parents should set aside their differences for the welfare of the children. Phrases from the judge like "these two parents need to learn how to get along here" are common. When the perpetrator hears that phrase, it is a clear message that the court does not understand the power he has over his wife. Thus, he feels empowered and emboldened. The words may actually encourage abuse of his power over his wife through the litigation of custody or control over finances. For certain, he knows how to gain control because he knows his wife's fears. In addition, he knows whether he has used the threat of taking custody of their children, as domestic abuse perpetrators often do to maintain control of their wives during the marriage.

To the domestic abuse victim, those same words from the judge's lips tell her that the court does not understand that the victim's husband cannot negotiate. His way is to demand compliance and capitulation, through the use of intimidation, violence, or threats. She knows that the only way to gain equality is for the court to have an understanding of her husband and to use the court's power to secure her equality. Thus, the victim is fearful and a sense of helplessness is heightened. She knows she may be at risk of more violence (Fox & Zawitz, 1999). This is the time for her to be hypervigilant. The victim sees the court as having the power over her husband that she does not have.

Before coming to court, she anticipates that the court will use its authority to protect her.

Domestic abuse–sensitive language can assure that both parents receive equal protection. The court can use its power to let the perpetrators and the victims know the long-term impact of violence in the home, and can speak directly to this issue. For example, a judge can state, "I hope you understand the importance of not trying to use the court to control your wife, as I will not tolerate it. The children need to be assured of that protection to the full extent of the law. The children may not have seen your violence to your wife, but they are victims of it nevertheless. Surely, your wife behaved differently than she would have had she not feared that you would continue to hurt her. If nothing else, the children are aware of that. They are entitled to two parents who are free from violence. I intend to . . ."

That same judge can look to the domestic abuse victim and state, "While I am aware of your husband's ability to control you or to try to use the court, it is also important for you to understand my role is to allow the children to have the best relationship they can with both of you. To that end, I ask you to try to overcome your fears in the presence of the children and for you to try to assist in the relationship with their father."

Such oratory signifies that the judge recognizes the perpetrator's power and ability to control and acknowledges the domestic abuse victim's difficulty to encourage a positive relationship with their father. In fact, to do so may not be a natural response for the domestic abuse victim. It also creates a new power structure for both parents, so that the victim can come back to court for assistance when she needs it. In addition, the husband-perpetrator knows that the court has and will use its power to continue to protect his abused wife.

Many states require parents to try to negotiate visitation schedules even where there has been a finding of domestic abuse. In that circumstance, it is imperative that a court communicate correctly and can tell both parents, "The children have already been hurt by being raised in a home where one parent fears abuse. I will use my power to keep that from happening again and to keep coercive parenting from being perpetrated on the children. This state takes seriously its obligation to protect children from emotional harm as well. Witnessing or experiencing verbal abuse, name-calling, or put-downs of the mother or the children will cause harm to the children, and this court will not permit that to occur. I am not discouraging negotiation, but I want this mother to know that the court is a friendly place to victims and I want this father to know that his parental rights do not give him the right to hurt their mother or create fear."

The message to the victim is, "If you are fearful or there are threats or you believe the children are at risk, I encourage you to tell your lawyer and to get assistance from this court." The same statement tells the perpetrator, "As already stated you will see your children and hopefully behave appropriately. But I will immediately stop contact until you learn to do so if I find out that berating or name-calling or threats are continuing."

Another common problem occurs during litigation over sole custody, as many states strongly encourage joint custody and joint decision making. It is illogical to believe that someone who has used coercion and threats as a manner of control will simply stop this behavior voluntarily. Nevertheless, courts too frequently lose sight of this aspect of human nature as it becomes impossible to negotiate with the husband-perpetrator. We have heard countless judges comment almost offhandedly with phrases such as, "If this woman wants to spend all the marital funds to litigate. . ." Each time we hear this we cringe. This phrase translates into a lack of consideration for a victim's inability to negotiate with her abuser. Such words also signify a failure to recognize the impact of domestic abuse on children.

Judges need to be particularly sensitive to the things they say, as their words may open the door for the perpetrator to repeat a phrase that was once used by the court any time the victim returns to court to seek relief. This same type of phrase is a put-down to the victim for her attempt to secure her children's best interests. In fact, under the Constitution parents are required to protect their children from harm. There is no qualification, for example, that the children will only be protected from strangers. If a parent truly believes the children need protection from a parent, or if the one parent uses the children as a weapon against the other, sole custody and decision making may be the required and desired custody order for that family. But when the victim who seeks sole custody in this circumstance hears a put-down by the court, the victim feels pressure to capitulate in order to avoid provoking the court's ire. This is true even when the mother truly believes sole custody is important. In fact, spending to protect children is a legitimate expenditure of marital funds. So when a judge makes negative comments about tapping those funds, it feels as if the judge is making a legally unfounded assertion that it is not legitimate to spend marital funds in this way.

Domestic abuse–sensitive language requires an understanding of the need for a domestic abuse victim to have financial independence in order to remove the perpetrator's control. It also requires the use of the court's contempt powers to assure the perpetrator's compliance with judicial orders that are issued because the court must be steadfast in its support for the victim. The abuser may disagree, but the court is required to enter orders regarding support and visitation that recognize that it is legitimate to expend a large amount of money to protect children.

The impact of language also is felt in how society views the separate parental roles of mothers and fathers. Fathers who seek custody are seen somehow as "noble" or "romantic" in trying to co-parent because some aspects of society still seem to give extra value to a father who wants to spend time parenting. On the other hand, some people expect the woman to want to parent. She receives no special recognition; it is her duty to parent. Where there is domestic violence, courts need to be sensitive to the fact that many fathers who spent little time with their child during the course of a marriage—such as taking the child to the doctor, helping with homework, encouraging friendships, knowing the child's friends, and seeking "quality time"—suddenly uses his goal of controlling his wife by seeking to take custody of the child from his wife, thereby endangering the child's security, social contacts, established routines, and emotional reliance on his protective mother. Accordingly, the seeming Santa Claus persona this father assumes in court regarding his interest in his child, in the context of domestic violence actually may have an ulterior purpose regarding the protective parent and a dissembling impact on the child's emotional security.

Domestic abuse–sensitive language would give a woman proper credit for the historically female job of raising the children and the difficult tasks ahead. In addition, such language would pierce any romantic notion about a father seeking to parent and instead look to the father's actual participation as a parent prior to the marital breakdown. Domestic abuse–sensitive language requires the recognition that the perpetrator is suspect for wanting to change the amount of time and responsibility from the level of participation he had prior to the divorce proceeding. Statements such as, "We should be happy he wants to spend time with the kids" or "Aren't the kids lucky to have a father willing to spend more time with them?" should be scrutinized.

Sensitivity to both parents and their children requires determining what the status quo was before the marital relationship came to court, because security for children includes ensuring that they experience the least amount of disruption to their lives. This is likely to mean enabling them to stay in the same home and school, maintain friendships, and have a similar amount of time with each parent so long as it is in a safe environment. A romantic view of the father's active parenting is not appropriate where there is domestic abuse. Language used by the court or experts that does not recognize the inequality of power and control between victim and the perpetrator is not domestic abuse–sensitive.

Frequently, issues of estrangement and accusations of alienation are rendered in court. Where an accusation arises in the context of a domestic abuse history, it is particularly important for the court to be sensitive to language. The starting point? The judge should question the parent who is alleging alienation or estrangement about the familial arrangement for child care prior to the breakdown of the marriage. If the mother was the children's primary caregiver throughout the marital relationship and there was domestic abuse, it seems appropriate for the victim to feel angry or outraged if a previously uninvolved father suddenly wants total or shared custody.

Courts may draw a negative inference if an alleged victim has never called the police about abuse. Instead, the court should ask a perpetrator, "Why now?" if he is seeking to spend more time with children. It is appropriate to suspect his motivation where there is a sudden shift. It must be considered as a part of a power and control issue. Where children are thriving with the status quo of the mother being primary custodian, a court needs to recognize that if the children are suddenly with the perpetrator at times when they were not with him during the marriage, it might be tolerable or even pleasant for them but it is not the status quo.

Frequently, courts view as negative a victim's appropriate anger at being victimized, instead of accepting anger as a natural consequence. The court should not use any punishment, reprisal, or angry language with a victim who is angry as a result of being a victim. Instead, sensitivity to her status as a victim includes determining whether she has a reasonable basis for her anger. Were a stranger to victimize, anger would be appropriate. If so, this same standard should be applied to victims of domestic abuse. Use of sensitive language requires thinking outside the realm of family court and an analysis similar to the stranger/perpetrator/victim model. For example, in criminal law we take victim impact statements and victims participate in plea negotiations because the victims' anger is accepted and understood as appropriate. In this way, the need to protect children from the abuser would be clear to anyone who hears the facts. Likewise, in entering visitation orders, the court should use the same analogy involving violence to a stranger in considering a child's reaction to a person they know to be capable of violence. Again, the need to protect the child would become obvious.

Frequently, the perpetrator uses *manipulative anger*. It is spoken in a manner designed to show that he is incredulous and indignant. We are reminded of a case where a child was abused in the attic of the family home. When the alleged perpetrator was asked about this, he denied ever going to the attic. If there was no abuse, why not state instead that he would never abuse a child? The nuances of such responses are important if courts are to be domestic abuse–sensitive.

Sometimes people do not understand why criminal charges are not brought where there has been violence to children. There is an assumption that criminal charges are not brought because the violence was not serious, but there are other more likely explanations. There is a difference between criminal and civil standards of proof. In addition, there are few women victims who want to put the father of their children in jail. A prosecutor has the discretion to decide not to bring charges. If a woman does not press charges, a prosecutor's decision not to file criminal charges is understandable.

Even where a judge is sensitive, there is the much-overlooked factor of judges handling as many as a thousand cases a year; there is little time for each case. In addition, whereas court orders are designed for finality, a family's needs are in flux, thus creating a dynamic between the court and the family that is inconsonant.

There have been many changes in the area of domestic abuse over the years. The importance of judicial sensitivity in the use of language in family court should not be underestimated.

[5]

UNDERSTANDING THE IMPACT
OF VIOLENCE ON CHILDREN

Courts should employ a child-centered, protective strategy in child custody cases involving allegations of child maltreatment and domestic abuse, and such a strategy must be grounded in a complete understanding of the impact of violence on children. Issues of child physical, sexual, or emotional abuse and domestic abuse frequently arise and remain during the pendency of custody and visitation litigation. Courts are confronted with having to make temporary awards of custody and orders regarding visitation, often on little evidence, long before either party puts on its complete case. Parents' constitutionally protected rights to due process and to parent one's children may compete with the welfare of the children and the need to balance the potential harms of erroneous decisions.

The policy mandate for reunification of the family outlined in various state statutes and often employed by both the courts and child protective service agencies foster a system that does not serve to protect children. These public policies and statutes should be reviewed and revamped as they relate to child protection regardless of whether custody is an issue before a court. But it is critical to understand them to know how to work effectively within the court system.

Previous public incidents, such as the death of Faheem Williams in Newark, New Jersey at the hands of his caregiver (and abuse of others in the family underscore that the child protective system is not working. In each of these cases, child protective services was involved but the system failed. Child protection policy needs to be examined as a public health concern and cannot be repaired in a piecemeal fashion. Numerous statutes make clear their intention to safeguard the emotional and physical welfare of its youngest citizens so that children's welfare is fully protected. Also, a state may make it possible for individuals with knowledge or information indicating that a child may be abused or neglected to file complaints for child protection.

Courts entrusted with overseeing the welfare of children can and should provide protection in the form of limited, supervised contact, or no contact on a temporary basis while allegations are investigated, even prior to a preliminary hearing in child custody/visitation cases. Thus, public policy considerations for preservation of the emotional and physical health of the child may foreclose a parent from co-parenting or having any contact with the potentially offending parent or guardian. States would then be affording child victims the identical relief from the perpetrator that is often given to adult victims of family violence under domestic abuse statutes.

Domestic abuse laws throughout the country recognize that violence is a serious crime against society. Many have policies recognizing a correlation between adult family violence and child abuse. It is well understood that children, even when they are not physically assaulted, suffer serious emotional effects from exposure to family violence. Domestic abuse statutes often permit the granting of temporary relief to adults without notice to the offending adult because of the great risk understood to be involved where there is domestic abuse. Thus, to give children this identical relief is appropriate.

There are also laws that recognize the dangers posed to children by the potential for recidivism by sex offenders and other offenders who commit predatory acts against children. Sex offender registry systems have been created to assist in the protection of children. These acts recognize the significant devastating effects on children when perpetrators of sexual violence are parents of the child. All states make it a crime if a parent causes or permits a child to engage in a prohibited sexual act or other sexually prohibited and offensive acts. Thus, whoever the state charges with child protection must act in concert with all statutes designed to protect children and ensure their best interests are preserved.

Issues of abuse arise in several ways. They may arise in the context of domestic abuse and custody/visitation disputes, or they may be brought to the attention of the courts by an abuse complaint through an agency designed to protect children. Parents or other persons interested in the child may originate an abuse and neglect case on behalf of a minor child. That is, schools, state agencies, mental health professionals, and other individuals may bring neglect or abuse of children to the attention of the agency, and in many states can file an abuse and neglect complaint in court as an interested party.

In stark contrast to the aforementioned policies and laws is the policy often enunciated by custody laws and requirements for judicial decision making in child custody cases. These considerations often require a court to ensure frequent and continuing contact with both parents after the parents have separated or dissolved their marriage, and express public interest to encourage parents to share the rights and responsibilities of child rearing. This is so even where domestic abuse has been recognized and adjudicated. Although the safety of the child or parent from the physical abuse of the other parent, history of domestic abuse (if any), and parental fitness are often among the factors that must be considered by trial courts in making a custody determination, the paramount concern for safety of the child is conspicuously absent and may even appear to be overwritten in the requirements as it regards custody and visitation decisions. There is a fundamental legal principle that requires that laws be construed so as to not conflict with each other. To enforce this policy would require courts to apply the protective public policies to child custody and visitation cases. Thus, when a parent's right to have access to his or her child is in conflict with the child's need for safety from that parent, the child's need for safety should take precedence. Until policy is altered to make clear that protection of children in all contexts from abuse, violence, and neglect is critical to promote their best interests, and policy and laws are set forth to make clear that the safety of children is the mandate of child protective services and the court, the system fails our youngest citizens and compromises their welfare.

Children, having no power of their own, must rely on the state in its role as *parens patriae* to secure those rights, afford them those protections, and safeguard their welfare. To give meaning to the notion of prevention from abuse, the right of children to be safe and secure in their homes should be given more weight than the weight of a parent's right to raise them. However, the underlying premise in many statutes is that the children's best interests lie in their return to their home. Perhaps the underlying question should be: What can the agency do to secure a child's rights to be safe and secure and to prevent that child from suffering future physical or emotional abuse?

Parents who allege victimization of themselves or their children before or during custody or visitation litigation frequently run into a wall of disbelief from the child protection system, legal system, and even their own attorneys. Many victims of domestic abuse will not disclose their experiences or their fears for their children out of concerns for retaliation by the batterer, shame, or a belief that they will not be believed and might even lose their children. Trial courts must determine the custody/visitation plan that serves the best interests of the child by considering a number of factors. The trial court may also consider any other facts or conditions determined to be relevant to the unique facts of the individual case. Upon the initial raising of child abuse or maltreatment allegations to the trial court in a custody/visitation matter, numerous protections afforded victims and children of parents who are victims of domestic abuse are not reiterated in all custody statutes.

Even where statutes do not provide specific procedures for the court to follow when allegations of child maltreatment are alleged in a divorce action, procedures for abuse should be followed. The court has the authority to make findings as to the occurrence of child maltreatment by a parent and can make such findings at preliminary stages of a custody proceeding in order to ensure the safety of the child.

There is no reason for a court to treat allegations of child maltreatment or domestic abuse raised in a custody case differently from those brought before it by an agency of child protection. The risks of harm to a child whose abusive parent continues to have access are known and are no less severe because they are raised in the context of a custody dispute. If similar sworn-to allegations made by a parent or guardian would warrant the court's removal of a child from a parent pursuant to child protective laws, the identical remedy should be afforded the child and imposed by the trial court in the context of a custody/visitation action. The child's safety should be no less guaranteed. By construing the custody statute in light of the principles and procedures outlined in child welfare laws and domestic abuse statutes, children will be assured more protection and their best interest more certain.

Under custody statutes, proof of the occurrence of child maltreatment or domestic abuse is generally a subsidiary fact that contributes to the court's conclusions about factors such as parental fitness. These factors themselves are subsidiary findings that form the basis for the trial court's determination of the ultimate issue—the best interests of the child. To ensure best interests of a child, the fact of abuse and its impact on the child is what is critically relevant.

Concerns of child abuse and domestic abuse are not less likely to be unfounded when first raised in the context of custody/visitation. Protections against domestic abuse should not end because someone is in a custody or visitation dispute. In fact, in some states domestic abuse restraining orders, once granted, cannot be removed by motion of an abuser without going before the court and demonstrating good cause for dissolving the order. It is irrelevant to child protection whether domestic abuse is raised before, during, or after a divorce. Whenever domestic abuse is found, a court can never lose sight of the fact that each time the parties are before it, there is a perpetrator and a victim. The right to due process does not alter the basic fact that a victim and perpetrator are before the court, even long after a restraining order has been granted. In some states harassment is given equal effect as violence. It is incompatible for a court to consider a parent's ability to communicate and cooperate in matters relating to the child where there has been family violence or child abuse. We would no more require a victim of stranger violence to communicate after an attack than we would require a child victim of sexual assault by a stranger to face that abuser again. Many states mandate mediation except where there is domestic violence for this very reason. It is understand that there should be no direct communication between a victim and his or her abuser: mediation requires equal power and a victim does not have equal power.

Domestic violence–sensitive knowledge and language by the court is imperative, not just at a domestic abuse hearing but even years later, as these matters may continue to be before the courts. For example, while it may be ordinary for a judge in a custody/ visitation dispute to attribute wrongdoing equally for engaging in divorce litigation, it is an error to do so where there has been a finding of domestic abuse. When equal blame is attributed in the face of domestic abuse, the motivation of perpetrators to use child custody litigation as yet another way to control and intimidate their victims is reinforced and unwittingly sanctioned by the court. No victim of stranger violence would be required to schedule visitation or be expected to speak with that individual to work out anything at any time. Yet picture a scenario in which an abuser has threatened to kill a domestic abuse victim or her children, and the victim is later seen as recalcitrant if she resists working out visitation issues during a divorce. While judges wonder why a victim is still saying she is frightened when there has been no incident of violence in a long time, scenarios such as this are a daily occurrence in family courts.

The constitutionally protected right of citizens to parent is derived from the court's judicial gloss placed on the privacy rights implicit in the First Amendment (religion, free exercise, speech); the Fourth Amendment (right to be secure in their persons and houses); the Fifth Amendment (no deprivation of life or liberty without due process); and the Ninth and Tenth Amendments (enumeration of certain rights, no denial of other rights retained by the people, and powers not delegated . . . are reserved to . . . the people), all of which are secured through the Fourteenth Amendment, which places restriction on state action.

State legislatures can modify language to try to make a child's safety a serious concern, but so long as a child protective service agency is intertwined with maintaining parents' rights, it is difficult to unravel the inexorable problem: the conflicting nature of its dual mandate. As they stand now, these agencies tend to be responsible for monitoring themselves. Their function is to try to keep a family together and to reunify the family after its members have been separated, as well as assisting in plans for future child placement where a child is removed from the home. Ultimately, despite obligations to reunify the family, these same agencies may be designated as responsible for the care, custody, guardianship, maintenance, and protection of children.

Unfortunately, the message is that child safety is merely a concern to be considered, and this allows children to be placed at risk. It is a challenge for child service agencies to be expected to both promote reunification and child protection simultaneously, just as it would be challenging for a prosecutor to defend someone who is being prosecuted. Moreover, legislation does not have specific standards to ensure prevention of further injury while facilitating the goal of maintaining the familial relationship. It is axiomatic that the best predictor of future behavior is past behavior. If a parent harmed a child, the child is at risk of harm with that parent in the future.

In 2002, the New Jersey Division of Youth and Family Services (DYFS), closed the case of a child who killed another child. DYFS, New Jersey's child protective service agency, had provided services and counseling to this family. Clearly it was not enough. Did they see the abuse in the family? Was a child mimicking a parent? Did the child really need to die? In this case, the dichotomy was clear: the child was not truly paramount and risk of harm was tolerated.

The language often used by judges flows naturally from the requirements of our custody statute regarding equal access and other provisions. It may also result from a bias that because violence has occurred in a family setting, its impact is less severe or less traumatic. When a court does this it is actually placing the setting of the family ahead of the presenting issue. For example, when a victim of domestic abuse or a protective parent hears admonishments by the court regarding failure to communicate with her abuser about a child or her unwillingness to cooperate with visitation plans she believes are dangerous to herself and the child, the victims hears the message that her victimization and that of her child are not believed or not worthy of the court's concern. Under these circumstances, a victim may be inhibited and intimidated and may fail to present her concerns to the court. The perpetrator hears the same admonishments to the victim and may feel empowered. The net effect is to neutralize and disregard the victims' very real experiences of violence and the effect of such violence on their functioning, leaving victims at risk for further harm. Instead, the court should be mindful of the potential that a perpetrator may use custody/visitation as a continuing means of control against his victim(s).

Divorcing parties are sometimes referred to as warring parties. No criminal court would think of a victim and her assailant as warring parties when in court, regardless of how many years before the assault had occurred. A teller who robbed a bank would never be told not to rob again and be allowed to go back to work as a teller. Yet every day judges permit batterers to return to work as parents, requiring child victims to visit with a parent who perpetrated domestic abuse on their mothers. It is just as unthinkable to require parents to agree and cooperate, or to ensure frequent and continuing contact with both parents, when there has been domestic abuse. It is incredible that courts too often do not make that distinction. Every day, parents who are victims of violence are required to send their children to be with their abuser. Court action too often punishes the child's protective parent for its overcrowded calendar. A victim of violence in family court may be sanctioned if she fails to send a child who witnessed this assault to visit with the perpetrator. This is true even if the child does not want to go. In part, this happens because the court has not integrated the language of conflicting public policies, and in part because a parent's right to parent is protected. Frequently, judges express more outrage at the impact of a child not seeing a parent than they do to the impact of the abuse. Evaluators sometimes accuse these parents of non-existent syndromes and judges rely on their assertions prior to trial, sometimes expounding that the mere separation between parent and child causes serious damage to the parent child relationship, all the while ignoring the damage done to the child by the abuse.

The protective parent is accused and blamed by the courts for creating a rift between the abusive parent and the child witness or victim of violence. Little or no attention or blame is placed on the offending parent because their parental rights are at stake. In doing this, the child's rights and need for protection may get lost.

More than sensitive language is required. Competent risk assessments should be mandated. Family court judges have the authority to order risk assessments. Well-trained professionals should only do these assessments with adequate knowledge of family violence and its impact, and they should make recommendations without regard to the welfare of anyone but the child being assessed. Such risk assessments should be routinely done by well-trained experts when domestic abuse is raised. In addition, a similar approach should be used when the allegations concern child maltreatment of any type, since ongoing visitation between the perpetrator of child abuse and the child victim can result in ongoing victimization and intensified trauma. Continuing use of risk assessments during custody/visitation litigation, even long after a violent act, would be another way for a court to convey to the parties its recognition of the long-term impact of domestic abuse.

Proof of parental unfitness may require not only establishing that the parent engages in violent or threatening behaviors or cannot parent because of a mental illness or substance abuse problems, but also that the parent's conduct has a substantial adverse effect on the child. Statutory and regulatory provisions that remove discretion by the judge should be promulgated to ensure that knowledge of the impact of such abuse on a child with the public policy of child safety is the court's chief concern. Accordingly, if the standard of proof is met, then the proof itself should be sufficient to assume adverse effect. To do otherwise makes a mockery of clear and stated public policies.

Most victimized children are harmed by their parent or parents, yet much child maltreatment goes unreported and undetected (Child Welfare Information Gateway, 2015). All forms of child maltreatment—physical abuse, sexual abuse, neglect, and psychological maltreatment—harms children, and may do so permanently. For these reasons, it is critical that courts take actions to minimize the risk of harm to children who are caught in custody disputes. The first step is to take actions to protect vulnerable children.

Although visitation between a child and parent is considered to be a fundamental right, this right can be and should be abrogated when initial evidence shows that such contact poses a danger or a risk of danger to the emotional or physical health and safety of the child. There is no known psychological profile of a parent who causes physical injury to a child. Abusive parents are in every culture and social strata of our society. Regardless of the background of the particular perpetrator, procedures in place by the child protective and domestic abuse statutes should be required to be followed in custody/visitation matters whenever these issues are raised by a parent.

Sometimes child abuse is part of a pattern of family violence in a home. The presumption should be that victims should be initially be believed and supported by the court with adequate protections imposed. If child protective measures imposed by child protective statutes were required to be used by courts, then financial disequilibrium of the family would be less relevant and the other issues in the family circumstance could be acknowledged without putting the children at further risk.

While much has been made in recent years of the supposed high frequency (Forssell & Cater, 2015) of allegations of sexual abuse in child custody cases, such allegations are raised in a very small percentage of contested custody cases. However, these cases frequently garner a disproportionate share of attention and resources (Tjaden & Thoennes, 2000; Trocme & Bala, 2005).

In addition, false allegations occur in these custody cases at a rate similar to that in cases of sexual abuse in general. In New Jersey, for the purpose of Family Court cases, sexual abuse of a child renders the child an "abused child" when the abuse is committed by or allowed to be committed by a parent, guardian, or other person having custody and control of the child. Unlike other forms of child maltreatment, the perpetrator of sexual abuse may already have a relationship of trust and acquiescence with the victim.

Because there is no way to predict which children will suffer to what degree, and because the use by an adult of his or her inherently more powerful position to exploit a child is wrong and sometimes criminal, prompt and complete protection must be afforded to these victims. Protective parents should not have to fear that a court will be skeptical because issues of sexual abuse arise during litigation. The court in a custody/visitation matter should integrate all of the protective policies available whether a parent files a specific and separate abuse complaint or not.

Visitation between a child and parent is considered to be a fundamental right that can be abrogated only when such contact poses a real danger to the emotional or physical health and safety of the child. Given the broad discretion of the court that hears a child custody matter, a wide array of potential actions are available, including court-ordered risk assessments, supervised visitation, no-contact orders, appointment of counsel for the child, and so on. All of these actions are consonant with protecting child victims. When courts further integrate this public policy stance with state of the information concerning the debilitating effects of exposure to violence and maltreatment, the rationale for limited, supervised contact or no contact between a perpetrator and his or her child victim becomes obvious.

The detrimental nature of contact when a child has been emotionally, physically, or sexually injured by a parent, at least until the child is healed and feels fully protected and safe, should be assessed by the court no differently than it would be with stranger violence. It is only with the actual implementation of all policies designed to protect children, together with the vast knowledge available to our courts, that children's best interests will be protected in the context of custody and visitation disputes.

Unfortunately, even when child protection comes before parental rights, a child may still go unprotected. Consider the case in which an agency is involved but does not substantiate abuse or does not seek court intervention. Assume further that for any number of reasons, an investigation is improperly done. Investigatory and decision-making powers of child protective agencies are broad and blind from public review. There is little ongoing public accountability.

One must wonder whom this policy is protecting. The most fundamental rights of due process are at issue when a protective parent disputes a finding of "not substantiated," which then is relied upon by the court and the case is subsequently dropped. The adversary system requires opposing positions to have information and to be able to challenge available information. Cross-examination is said to be the "searchlight for the truth." When a complaint of abuse is actually filed, law guardians often rely on agency investigations. So they too go unchecked. As long as these investigations are not subject to public scrutiny, flaws are less likely to be found and challenged. Abuse can be prevented if agencies are open to better oversight and required to have competent and knowledgeable professionals charged with assisting the court to recognize and understand the early impact of psychological and physical abuse of children.

A critical issue in highly publicized cases is the inability to ascertain that the children were at risk or abused. The knowledge and training of professionals able to substantiate abuse when there are no physical findings is paramount. Legislatures have the capacity to require use of trained professionals who are able to substantiate abuse based on known psychological data and what is known about family violence.

Sometimes the system may fail because of a lack of knowledge and expertise. In the New Jersey case of *Gubernat v. Deremer*, the Supreme Court held that the child's last name should not be based on a historical bias toward the father's surname. Rather, the best interest of the child should be examined. The child's mother, who was the custodial parent and primary caregiver, won the right to the child's surname, but the father killed the child and himself just days later. This child need not have died had someone understood, recognized, and appropriately dealt with the father's abuse.

In New Jersey, the Domestic Violence Act has mandated ex parte relief for victims of domestic abuse; the policy is maximum protection for victims. This statute recognizes that even when they are not directly victims of abuse, children suffer long-lasting effects from living in a home where domestic violence exists. That statute also recognizes a positive correlation between spousal abuse and child abuse. Nevertheless, the legislature has fallen short of providing children the same protections afforded the adult by way of relief from contact with that parent. To enjoin a parent from contact with a child should be no more or less stringent. In seeking restraining orders a party must establish (a) the likelihood of irreparable harm; (b) that the applicable law is well-settled; (c) that the material facts are not substantially disputed; (d) that she will likely prevail on the merits; and (e) that the hardship on the non-movant does not outweigh the benefit to the movant. However, when a child is in need of injunctive relief for his or her safety and well-being, the same standards do not apply. Rather, the state's strong public policy and mandate to preserve and foster the family unit requires children to meet a much higher standard. To stop contact between a parent who may have abused a spouse or a child in that context contradicts the state policy assumption that contact between child and parent promotes the welfare and growth of that child. Nevertheless, suspension of contact between a child and a parent to prevent abuse and neglect should not undergo a more rigorous test than would be required to enter any injunction under the Domestic Abuse Act. But no such law exists to protect children and provide restraining orders for children.

In all states, safety is supposed to be the paramount concern for children. State agencies are supposed to promote their safety. But sometimes they are asked to do conflicting things. How can one agency operate under two directives? How can the agency designed to reunite families be the same agency that is supposed to be there to protect children? Might not such an agency's directives conflict at times? And when it does, does children's safety play second fiddle to reunification of the family?

[6]

THE ATTORNEY-CLIENT INTERVIEW

Its Importance and Implications

The initial interview defines the attorney-client relationship. Both individuals meet to make a decision. The litigant seeks to hire someone to represent her legal interests. She must trust that the person she chooses will do so with understanding and integrity. The lawyer she chooses will set the course for the litigation that follows. She will be paying for an expensive service. She must be certain that the attorney not only knows the law, but also understands the nature of abuse. The attorney must be sympathetic to her, yet guide with confidence.

The attorney must also decide whether or not to represent an individual. Most of us in the matrimonial field find the practice stressful by the very nature of the emotional issues. Therefore, it is most important to choose clients with whom a rapport develops. Sometimes battered women can be reserved, other times overly controlling. Attorney may find the latter intrusive and reject a client for that reason.

There are five basic concerns every litigant should satisfy when choosing an attorneys to be engaged in a divorce/custody dispute where domestic abuse has been present: knowledge, trust, strategy, communication, and money.

In domestic abuse cases, knowledge of the law is only the first step. Except where there is a domestic abuse restraining order, even an abusive spouse may share the marital residence during the divorce litigation. Thus, if the spouse is abusive but there is no protective order, the prospective attorney must know the circumstances under which a protective order can be obtained and explain that to the client. Whether or not to seek a protective order may be a strategy, but it should never be done absent legitimate circumstances and fear.

One of the most important lessons for an attorney is that because the abusive relationship is about power and control, the denial of a restraining order sought by a litigant may have a devastating effect on the litigant. The abuser will feel empowered and he may do subtle and overt things to hurt the wife or the children. A litigant's reactions may have an effect on the attorney. If she responds in a way the attorney does not agree with or understand, he might find it frustrating and time consuming. Child custody cases are labor intensive and require patience.

If the case is already in litigation, it is important to find out why the woman is dissatisfied with her attorney, and to make certain that her issues will be dealt with satisfactorily. This is the basis of building a trustful relationship.

Assuming the attorney and client are mutually comfortable, all the information necessary to proceed is ascertained during one or more interviews, and a strategy must be developed. An assessment must be made as to the impressions the court already has about the client, her husband, as well as the needs of the children. The entire file must be read with skepticism. Try to figure out what is missing from the court's opinion of the client that needs to be changed.

At each step communication is essential. The basis of every battering relationship is a relationship in which love and trust were exploited. Open communication helps build trust. Issues should be discussed until there is an understanding between the client and the attorney. This communication must be an ongoing and integral part of the litigation process as new issues arise.

The ability to financially afford the litigation is an important factor to be considered. Trust, communication, knowledge, and strategy may all be present, but without adequate financial arrangements litigation becomes stifled. Failure to abide by the terms of an agreement may create a conflict of interest that requires the attorney to file a motion with the court to withdraw from representation. This can hurt a client. On the one hand, it is the attorney's responsibility, to the extent possible, to keep the client apprised of the financial impact on the case of differing strategies and actions. On the other hand, the client must recognize that the attorney is engaged in this as work and expects to be paid. This needs to be discussed openly. When money becomes a problem between the client and the attorney, communication and trust can easily break down.

Repeatedly, we see mental health professionals without adequate training in child abuse or custody issues in general, and without being familiar with information developed from critical attorney-client interviews, giving "expert testimony" based on scientifically unfounded theories. The disheartening result is that the concerns of protective parents are ignored and children are placed in the custody of abusive parents. We would like to raise some questions about how the mental health professions might assure that their members offering expert testimony in family court have the requisite education and experience to make evaluations and recommendations that are in children's best interests.

Josh Powell murdered his children while he was at the center of a criminal investigation for his wife's disappearance and likely murder (Miller, 2014). We do not believe that any judge ever expects the case before him will eventuate in the death of a child or a spouse. No judge expects a Josh Powell. No judge in a divorce action ever expects a respected member of the community to be a Jerry Sandusky and to have abused his or others' children. But similar perpetrators are before judges every day, getting away with crimes against children. Mental health professionals play a critical role, since judges rely upon their expertise when they enter orders with regard to children.

The courts do not have expertise in the many areas of science, and so they rely on the testimony of "expert witnesses." The court places great reliance upon mental health professionals to assist in making decisions about the welfare of a child. What the professional opines often becomes the law of the case, and it becomes difficult, if not impossible, for either parent to overcome during the pendency of a case.

Mental health professionals have an immense share of the power in how the courts succeed or fail in protecting the welfare of children. The mental health professions have a responsibility to maintain standards of practice for its members who testify in child abuse and custody cases. During any divorce in any state in this country, children's best interests are supposed to be preserved. Too often, best interest gets turned on its head where there are allegations of abuse during divorce. It is here that mental health professionals play a critical role in assisting the court, and great reliance is often placed upon them. Because of this crucial role, they should never overstep their actual expertise, training, and experience.

It is difficult to enforce ethical guidelines, and sanction by professional associations has little legal force. Would it be feasible for licensing boards to create mechanisms for accountability, perhaps to craft rules and regulations that forbid their members from making recommendations to the court outside their expertise? Without such restrictions, professionals often proffer unfounded opinions in court that can promote harm to the very children who are the subjects of their evaluations. At present, under the rules of court, anyone with more than a layperson's knowledge may be permitted to testify as an expert.

Unless the mental health professions prohibit testifying outside one's expertise, rather than merely giving guidance through guidelines, there is no way to safeguard children's best interests through psychologists' and social workers' custody evaluations.

Children have few rights except as interpreted by a particular judge in a divorce action. Therefore, it is crucial that experts are trained and knowledgeable in all of the areas in which they are opining. Still, too many mental health professionals accept the designation as court-appointed expert without actually knowing the science of abuse.

Even when expert testimony includes misinterpretation of science or conjecture, it is still relied upon as fact by the court, often resulting in depriving the protective parent of custody. Made-up syndromes and other theories of conjecture are often used as though they were relevant to determining whether or not a child has been abused. These self-identified experts fail to testify that the best way to determine abuse is through an interview with the child; neither do they testify that accepted practice does not require an interview with the accused parent. It is well settled that interviews and examinations of the children themselves are the best determinants for whether or not abuse has occurred (Faller, 2015). Professionals who raise these alternatives often disparage the child's own voice and the accuracy of a child's report of abuse.

In the process, community scientific standards for determining abuse get pushed aside.

As a policy matter, professionals can influence the courts to prevent accusations that divorcing parents who raise questions of abuse are alienating or causing estrangement. Such accusations are conjectural. They become attacks against the protective parent's character and have no bearing, for example, on whether the accused parent has harmed the children. Most children do not lie about being abused by a parent. Yet frequently, mental health professionals who do not know this give opinions in court on these matters.

Mental health professionals have a duty to practice only within the scope of their training and experience. Yet without some means of establishing their expertise to testify on these matters, there is no way for the profession to maintain a high standard of conduct. Because lawyers take cases as advocates and are not experts in all fields of practice, and because there are many cases put forth by pro se litigants (acting as one's own advocate), it is important that mental health professionals themselves play a role in oversight. Licensing boards could regulate this through the passage of strict regulations whereby mental health professionals must establish that they have the relevant credentials before they are permitted to testify in specialized areas.

As things stand now, family courts believe that children have their safety needs met in the center of custody litigation between parents—often between parents of unequal power. When a parent raises the question of abuse after a disclosure of abuse by a child, the divorce court is the perfect setting for "attack dog" litigation—the protective parent becomes the target of attack, and the child's disclosure is attributed to the parent. The abuse issue often gets merged into the custody litigation as though it were a part of the custody matter. While guidelines for custody evaluations provide standards for forensic work and testimony, the means for enforcing these standards have not been adequate to protect children. The child has no right to appeal absent permission of the court. Children cannot object to any order affecting them, and they have no absolute right to cross-examine or seek redress of grievances as granted to them as citizens by the First and Fifth Amendments. Thus, without an expert holding to a rigorous standard prior to conducting a forensic evaluation, the courts merely have the lawyers or a pro se litigant asking questions. This leaves too much room open for children to go unprotected when they need protection. Our courts essentially seize young children without regard for their will and without standing to object, and they send them to be battered. This can be stopped if mental health professionals are willing to step forward to create and enforce specialized rules to apply to these cases.

There are social and cultural assumptions that need to be overcome in pursuing all claims, and mental health professionals who are properly trained can assist with these as well. For example, protective parents who bring the issue of abuse to the attention of a court are sometimes accused of attempting to get "a leg up" in a divorce or custody matter by raising child abuse. When the protective parent comes under scrutiny and the perpetrator named by the child is allowed to attack him or her, the court unwittingly exacerbates the abuse.

The change we need cannot be won in the courts on a case-by-case basis alone. No single story tells the world what parents trying to protect their children are facing daily in courts across the country. Protective parents are losing their children in custody cases while perpetrators gain the court's imprimatur to continue to abuse. The news media rarely cover abuse or custody cases unless there is a death. They shy from these cases, assuming them to be "he said, she said" stories. There is an expectation that if the court believed a child was abused, it would protect the child. After all, we live in a country that believes in and relies on its system of justice, so we assume justice must have prevailed or a bad parent would not have the custody of the children.

[7]

PLEADING THE CASE

The written information that is presented to the court on behalf of the victim is critical to the outcome of the case. Most importantly, it is crucial in the determination of interim decisions affecting custody and visitation.

In the area of domestic abuse, there are four general topics essential to good legal written work: knowledge of the law in the particular state and local jurisdiction; understanding the nature of abuse and the abusive power and control relationship (which includes the dynamic of what keeps a particular woman in a battered relationship); the characteristics of the battered spouse after she leaves the battering relationship; and the effects of domestic abuse on children.

A *pleading* is a document prepared by an attorney or litigant that is presented to the court, raising an issue for resolution by a court. The primary goal of a pleading is to properly raise a legal issue to place appropriate individuals and the court on notice of claims. Its purpose is also to put necessary information in front of the court so it can make knowledgeable determinations on interim issues.

The interim decisions made by a court are not normally based on the testimony of witnesses or experts. They are made by initial written pleadings. Therefore, how the information is prepared and what is chosen to be disclosed by the attorney or litigant is extremely important. These interim decisions are made upon presentations of certified or otherwise sworn to statements made by the litigants. In family court, parents who are the parties to an action are referred to as plaintiffs and defendants or petitioners and respondents. These are merely labels and are unimportant to the court in making decisions.

There are often other written papers, called exhibits, which are attached to the litigants' sworn statements. These exhibits are designed to corroborate the information being sworn to by the parent and may be reports from experts or certifications of witnesses, as well as other documents. Generally, the attorney prepares the pleading and the client reviews it and signs it, swearing to the truth of the information contained therein.

The first pleading presented in a divorce case is called a Complaint for Divorce. The legal response to a Complaint for Divorce is a pleading referred to as an Answer. If the person who submits or files an Answer also seeks a divorce for his/her reasons, they may submit or file a Counter-Claim for Divorce with the court. Most states do not require that both parties want a divorce. They may try to send the parties for counseling if it appears there is a chance for reconciliation.

A Complaint, Answer, and Counter-Claim places the legal issues of divorce at issue for the court to resolve. These documents, also known as "pleadings," do not raise specific temporary requests for relief, such as support, custody, or visitation. The pleadings designed to raise specific and interim legal issues are called Motions.

The issues raised by Motions must be supported by sworn statements called Certifications or Affidavits or other, similar terminology. A Motion is a pleading that requests specific relief from a court, such as child support or visitation. Along with the specific request is a sworn statement that contains the reasons as to why the relief should be ordered by the court. The court reviews the Motion, and sworn statement accompanying it, with its exhibits. It also reviews any responses filed by the other parent and enters an order. These orders become what is often referred to as "the law of the case" until there is a final disposition either by trial or by consent.

The final disposition can come through agreement of the parties or by the trial court. In either case the final order of the court is called a Judgment. A case technically ends with a Judgment. Between the filing of a Complaint and the Final Judgment there may be numerous issues upon which judges enter temporary orders.

In family law, custody and visitation are potential issues for resolution by the court until children are emancipated, that is, they become adults by virtue of age and independence or have a legal process that gives a teenager who is 16 or older legal independence from his or her parents or guardians. Thus, for the purposes of this book, there can be a final judgment that results in a divorce and final orders as to custody and visitation. Thereafter, the same process occurs with postjudgment litigation. So, for example, if a new issue is brought to a court's attention for resolution by the court after the divorce is final, it is similar to the first pleadings filed when a divorce is first initiated.

An attorney representing a battered spouse must be familiar with the laws protecting victims of abuse, as well as the custody laws. Knowledge of the law requires knowledge of the public policy concerns that the law is designed to safeguard.

Many battered women do not seek protective orders. Many do. In either case, the attorney must know the law, in the event a protective order becomes necessary during the pendency of a divorce and to properly plead the case. While domestic abuse laws act as instruments to provide protection to victims, laws contain language of legislative intent and public policy. Therefore, if a woman is battered but has not sought a protective order, the legislative intent and public policy decisions are also important to know.

The interplay of domestic abuse laws with custody laws is important. For example, someone may not have gotten a restraining order under a domestic abuse statute but might have been a battered spouse. Knowing that the intent of the domestic abuse law is to protect victims is important but may not seem relevant at first blush. But knowing that the law recognizes the long-lasting emotional impact on children, even when they have not been victims of violence, is imperative.

Battered women do not seek protective orders for many reasons. They are, however, concerned about their children and the impact of the abuser on their children. Just because a battered woman has not sought restraining orders, however, does not preclude telling the court, in detail, about the nature and extent of the abuse so that the victim's concerns for her children are placed in the correct context. The public policy concerns are designed to keep victims safe and give them protection, and they are present for everyone, not only those who seek protection. With many laws the legislature describes what its intent is before the actual legislation. It is often referred to as the "legislative intent," or a statement of "public policy." It is a statement of what is intended to be accomplished or achieved through legislation. It provides guidance to the courts to implement the legislation in accordance with the intent of the legislation. Unless the legislation is modified or interpreted by a court, the legislative intent, or public policy, must be followed. Therefore, even when a woman does not seek the court's protection, a court might be required to provide protection for her and the children because of legislative intent.

These policy issues should be considered and implemented by a judge when a litigant or attorney is unaware. The policies recognize the long lasting effects of domestic abuse upon children and directs the court to do everything possible to assure their safety. There are no caveats or loopholes. Thus, if a court were to be aware that the child witnessed domestic abuse, it should, *sua sponte* enter protective orders for the child. *Sua sponte* essentially means, "on its own," which is the language used when a court enters an order, without a request by a party. Rarely does this happen. Thus, it is up to the attorney to have the special knowledge and understanding of domestic abuse so the information can be proffered to the court in such a way as to request the court's recognition of the child in need of the court's protection.

All that is legally required in a Complaint for Divorce is to state a legal basis upon which a divorce may be granted pursuant to state law. For example, a divorce based on cruelty only needs to state that the spouse was cruel. However, in a case where there has been spousal abuse, especially where there have been threats that the abuser will seek custody, it is critical to state a detailed account of the history of the relationship, including the dynamics and abusive incidents and the fact that the abuser has threatened to take custody of the children.

Frequently, attorneys do not want to spend a client's money or their own time on the Complaint, since judges do not get to review the Complaints for Divorce when they are filed. The Complaint is merely an instrument that starts the process through a clerk, by which a state grants a divorce. It is the opening of the case. A Complaint may not even be read by a judge unless there is a trial. Only at trial must the court then know the grounds upon which the complaint is predicated. The court must then take testimony to ascertain whether the person has satisfied the particular requirements set forth in the law. Thus, attorneys need only state the grounds for divorce permitted in the law, and in the most general way. However, where there is abuse, the importance of an extremely detailed Complaint cannot be overstated.

Where there has been spouse abuse, specificity is essential, especially to prevail on a custody matter. Indeed, even during the pendency of a case a Complaint can be modified and submitted as an Amended Complaint. The Complaint with exhibits can ultimately become a roadmap for a trial.

It takes more time by the attorney in the beginning of the case, but a proper Complaint will save time and money during the course of litigation, where visitation or custody is anticipated to be a substantial issue. Information in the Complaint cannot properly be stated unless the attorney understands the relationship between the victim and the abuser. So, the interview upon which much of the Complaint is predicated must be supplemented with a detailed history garnered from a client's written statement of the history of the relationship. Anecdotal memories do fade, but may return in some detail when one is required to review one's own history,

The Complaint for Divorce is a critical document as it sets the backdrop of the case which will follow. Although the Complaint itself may not be read by the judge until the end of case, the facts encompassed in the divorce complaint may be referred to during the divorce, and portions of the complaint may become the basis for affidavits in support of a variety of motions regarding children. It will also be the first correct understanding and explanation of a spouse/victim's life of abuse. It is impossible to explain to someone else unless the attorney understands it. The Complaint is derived from a written history, and the initial client interviews are critical. Clients must give a detailed history of the relationship with their abuser. They must detail the relationship since the day they met. The attorney must understand the history as though they lived it. Specifically, an attorney should request that the client write as much detail as she can remember. Some attorneys suggest that clients only write on two-thirds of the right-hand side of the page. The left third of the page is reserved for dates and names of witnesses as they are subsequently recalled.

Attorneys should direct clients to write about how problems in the relationship were solved. It will help to explain the power dynamic in the relationship. The attorney needs to find out and understand what the mechanisms are in the relationship and find out how those mechanisms of control came about. The attorney must know the weaknesses of the victim as well as the client sees her own weaknesses. Remember, this is a woman who has been battered. Her view of the world may be skewed by her abuse and by the isolation which comes as a part of the abusive relationship. She may feel vulnerable and exposed and frightened of losing her children, for no reason which is apparent to the attorney.

The attorney must find out in what way the victim believes she is vulnerable. The abused spouse knows her abuser. She knows how he threatens and how he will try to hurt her through the courts. The attorney must understand her perspective and prepare the pleading using that knowledge to her advantage, while not leaving her open to attack for her known vulnerabilities. For more serious vulnerabilities, such as alcohol or drug abuse, one needs to be able to explain the circumstances that made her become dependent and show how removal of the abuse is aiding in her recovery.

The victim's ability to divulge her frailties and weakness is done in anticipation of an attack on her ability to parent. The victim may still be vulnerable to physical attack by her abuser and may drink to swallow her pain. Nonetheless, she may function, caring for children and the home, despite appearing frazzled. The abuser may go to work, keeping his job and status in the community. So when the victim goes public with her abuse, the images projected in public are jarring.

Despite all the publicity to the contrary, we expect someone who is labeled "abuser" to look like evil incarnate. When he dresses well, earns a lot of money, and is well-respected in the community, the picture does not mesh with our expectations. The wife does not necessarily show any bruises. Is she fabricating something up to get back at "him" for some reason? Is it easier to see her as vindictive rather than as a legitimate victim? We must paint an accurate picture when we go to court, before the court has an opportunity to make its own wrong judgment, based on what we all believe to be true about human nature, but which is false with a battering relationship.

For all the foregoing reasons, incredible detail, not usually necessary in a divorce, may become critical to explaining a domestic abuse relationship to the court. The key here is establishing an explanation in advance of a human judgment by the court and anticipating what abusers tend to do and how they continue to abusing the system. When one remembers that battering is about power and control, it follows that the batterer has an innate understanding of power. He will understand power within the court system and how to achieve power and undermine his wife's position in the court. By setting the stage accurately, with sufficient information, the victim's attorney is in a position to place information accurately and in the correct context before the court.

The victim's attorney must be strategic. The attorney should not file papers if those papers are expected to be "losers." Choose battles carefully. Every motion should state only provable facts, with exhibits attached as proofs.

The attorney must know anything that the husband knows about the wife's history such as prior sexual assaults and rapes, sexual abuse, alcohol abuse, drug abuse, physical violence, and her criminal history. Does she believe she yelled too much? Did she yell at the kids? Did she hit the children? Did she become so isolated that she dropped friends or relatives? Did she find herself alienated and alone? Why? Probe and learn. For example, if a woman has suffered depression and has been hospitalized, she may be embarrassed. The husband may have threatened to expose her depression to the court if she leaves him. He may have said he will tell the court everything, so that the court will find her an unfit parent and take her children away. This threat is designed to keep the woman in the marriage.

Similarly, the attorney must know that whatever mechanisms of control have been used to control the spouse are also likely to have been used with the children to control them. Victims must also detail the problems with the children.

Frequently, women believe the man will succeed and stay in the marriage. The attorney must understand why the woman stayed. Why does the woman believe he has the power to persuade the court and she does not? The attorney must be able to articulate the "hold" the abuser has/had on her. The abusing men persuaded their wives to marry and remain in the marriage. The men persuaded them that they were good people, providers, and fathers. To be an effective advocate the attorney must understand, in this particular woman's particular circumstance, why she could not, and did not, leave the marriage.

Among the most profound examples of domestic abuse are those in which the woman committed to marriage long before they really felt ready. She liked, or even loved, the man. Too soon, she agreed to marry. This may be the first indication he knows he can control her behavior with a threat. Does this sound benign? If instead of the threat he had merely proclaimed his love and desire for marriage, one might agree. The key was the threat to end a new relationship for no apparent reason. It is the first incident of control and being controlled. At the time, however, most women do not see that they are being controlled. They see themselves compromising, as loving. Nevertheless, the act of agreement, when it is against a person's true feelings and interest, is appeasement.

Over time, this mechanism continues. The man demands. The woman appeases. One day she attempts to assert her feelings on an issue. The man becomes angry. She does not do what he wants. He demands compliance. She refuses. He threatens her with something she fears. She complies. Time goes by. She continues complying with his demands. At some point his anger escalates. He threatens. And then it happens. She does not back down and continues to assert a position about something in an argument. He walks out, refuses to talk, and withdraws all affection for a day or two or a week. He finally begins to communicate as if nothing happened. Time passes. The issues do not get raised until something again comes up. This time she fears his threats or his walking out or his withdrawal of love and affection. She appeases but also tries to assert herself. He subtly threatens her. She knows what it means. She backs off and things quiet down. He says he's sorry and won't do it again. And then something clicks. This time there is no threat. He hits her and walks out.

She is angry and hurt. She wants to leave the marriage. She will not tolerate being hit. But their baby was just born. She is embarrassed to tell her family. Maybe she was silly for asserting herself. If she hadn't started the fight he would not have hit her. She knows he will calm down and come home. He does. He says he's sorry. He begs forgiveness and promises he will never do it again. She believes him and loves him. They are a family. They make love. Life continues as before. And so goes the pattern.

Eventually, isolation will become deep rooted. She feels relieved. He didn't hit her. He merely demanded compliance. She gives in. He tells her that it is much better for them to be alone— for her not to go out in the world. He tells her that their child needs her at home and that he needs her at home. She feels loved and desired and wanted. She complies. She has begun to set her "self" aside for the benefit of her husband but to her own detriment.

She does not even have time to attend to herself, as the child is upset. She ignores her own feelings and when he comes home, she apologizes for upsetting him and promises never to do it again. The twist has begun. She has now fully blamed herself for his bad behavior. He says he is sorry and life continues. Or, he doesn't say he is sorry and life continues.

This pattern of abuse escalates until the abuser has his demanded control and power over the victim. It only started because he wanted to be married. Is it still so benign?

To reiterate, this pattern must be understood in each case, with each of its specific and unique circumstances, and how it fits the general characteristics of the pattern of abuse. The keys to look for in the history are instances where the woman puts aside her own feelings or thoughts to do what her partner wants, even when it doesn't feel right. Quickly, the victim's goodwill is exploited. In the earlier example, for instance, the woman later feels embarrassed to tell family and friends that she did not really want to be married. The family may think her husband is a nice guy or they may have spent large amounts of money on the wedding party and she may fear they will be angry with her.

The damage here is that once she starts to live the lie, it is extraordinarily difficult to stop it. When a woman half-heartedly agrees to marry, she inadvertently gives up her independent decision making.

This is yet another example of an abusive relationships starting by the abuser exploiting a woman's goodwill or love. If the woman later does not want to do something the man wants her to do, she feels guilty. He accuses her of not loving him. She tries to prove her love. To do so she must put aside her feelings again. The cycle begins when she tries to appease him when he is angry. She tries to prove herself, but it is never enough. In between episodes, he apologizes and woos her back.

Children quickly learn what makes their parents angry and upset. If the parents use corporal punishment, the children know what provokes a spanking or some other punishment. Children hear a violent parent and quickly learn they are capable of violence, and they know what precedes the violence in the home. Did the woman serve mashed potatoes when he wanted baked? Did she walk too slowly to get him his coffee? Did she wear makeup or not wear makeup? Did he think she was too friendly, or not friendly enough?

Children know the abuser and know to be afraid that the abuse can turn on them if they create a circumstance where the abuser is provoked. Naturally, children want to avoid violence and do everything they can to appease the abuser. They also love him and want his approval. The combination is problematic because the victims know that their children understand that they have been unable to protect them. In anticipating a custody dispute an attorney needs to try to mitigate the control of the abuser at the outset of litigation. This can happen through openness and dealing with him as one would deal with a bully on the playground. Depending on the client, an attorney may suggest there be no verbal discussions between the parties. Rather, everything should be done by email—in some cases pre-approved by the attorney.

The court must understand the need for protection before it will order protection. If, for example, the husband threatened to withhold support if the wife left him, then the threat needs to be stated in advance of the request for monetary relief. Perhaps instead of asking that the husband be responsible to pay the bills, the attorney should ask for a necessary amount of money to the wife so she can pay the bills. That way, she will know if the bills are paid and not find herself in the dark when the electricity gets shut off. If he does not pay, she can seek enforcement in the court before there is such an emergency.

If no family history is presented, the court will not know what it needs to know. Regarding visitation, on the one hand, if a wife asks to limit visitation but gives no background of the dynamics of the abuse and how it relates to the child, the judge will have no reason to limit visitation. On the other hand, if the judge does not limit visitation but she articulates concerns, a history of abuse, and a child witnessing abuse, at least the court has been apprised, so that if problems arise with visitation, her story has been consistent and is credible. If she has not raised concerns early on, it is more difficult to explain the problems later on as being anything other than normal problems that kids or separated parents are likely to suffer.

Once a woman gets the strength to leave the relationship, her fear of her abuser does not go away. The attorney must give guidance. The woman does not trust, yet she needs to trust her attorney. She may resent the attorney if the court does not have an accurate understanding of what she has gone through. She may be demanding of the attorney's time. She may call too often. She may not call enough. She may appear angry. Or she may be compliant and then in a rage, unstable. In fact, she may need therapy.

Disclosing in writing the very information she fears the abuser will disclose removes some concern about how the information is revealed, since she is revealing it herself. The wind is taken out of the abuser's sails. He may still try to accuse her of unfitness, but she has already described the depression, the hospitalization, and anything else about herself. As we have been emphasizing, the best defense is to expose in advance. Be prepared to deal with these disclosures later so that they do not deflect from the real concerns before the court. Abusers are masters of deflection. Often their story sounds so logical; it is imperative to undo all the historical cobwebs. If the initial statement made by the husband is a lie, what follows cannot be the truth.

A lawyer must do the untwisting. For example, get the wife's medical records. Get releases to speak with her doctors. Get a written statement from a treating doctor that she is competent to parent, that her depression does not cause her to be a risk to her children. If possible, get a statement that shows she complained of being battered, emotionally or physically, or threatened. Back up incidents of abuse with police reports, if there are any, or medical reports to emergency rooms or doctor visits. If the wife was sent for psychological evaluations to experts before the divorce process began, be sure to get those reports. They can be used to show a court that the wife is stable and competent.

Victims of abuse know their abusers best. They know their threats and what threats are likely to be carried out. They know what information will be used about themselves against them by their spouse. An attorney needs to rely on the victims' concerns and to ask questions so that important issues are not overlooked.

Sexual violence is frequently an embarrassment. How many times have we had cases where women have had objects repeatedly thrust inside their rectums or vaginas? The embarrassment is overwhelming. They say it was against their will, that their husbands forced them. Will anyone believe them? They were a married couple. Unfortunately, even as they tell the story, or write it, the attorney must be acutely aware that most people find rape between married men and women incomprehensible.

Nevertheless, it is important to understand why the woman stayed in the marriage, as well the "hold" her spouse had, and still has, on her. The attorney must be comfortable with the explanations. A failure to do so means the explanations will not sound believable to anyone else. And, of course, in court, credibility is everything.

As circumstances evolve during a case, new issues involving the children may be brought to the court's attention for resolution. If an attorney enters a case with a history of domestic abuse during a time when a wife has visitation concerns, and the history of the violence has not been previously presented the court, it must now be done. At this juncture, it may also be important to enlist the assistance of an expert to put forth a position. Sometimes, the child may be having problems that may be difficult to understand. At those times, an evaluation may be an effective tool. In either case, the certification, which accompanies a request to modify, decrease, or negate in any way paternal control in the child's life, is going to have to be carefully explained or it will be seen by the court and exploited by the other side as an attempt to undermine the father-child relationship.

If the child is in therapy, contact with the therapist is important. If at all possible, it is helpful for the therapist to make a recommendation on behalf of the child's needs.

When the historical perspective has been ignored or understated, the attorney must go back through the history prior to litigation, as well as during the litigation, and explain the problems and use the assistance of an expert to help find a solution.

Essentially, the attorney must be able to convey a detailed understanding of the abusive spouse, what the abuser did, and the emotional scars that he left to both the victim and his children. These kinds of pleadings frequently take a long time to prepare. Between reading the history and integrating and talking to experts, and preparing historical exhibits, as well as the pleading itself, it is not unusual to spend 50–75 hours preparing a single pleading. The result is a very steep bill. But if the attorney fails to do this, it is difficult to make interim requests for modification, as the case will be ripe for the husband to attack the wife as the problem. When possible, an attorney should always have an expert opinion backing up the need for a modification in visitation. Then, if desired, a new evaluator can see what the problems were before the visitation modification and after the attorney's requested changes.

Again it goes to the knowledge of the effects of violence on children. All the pieces must be understood and integrated into each pleading by the attorney before it is presented to the court.

[8]

THE LITIGATION CONTINUED

The trial was over. It was humiliating. I sat on the witness stand. Sidney's attorney cross-examined me. I don't remember my own attorney asking me any questions. It was awful. I guess I must have testified that he was an insensitive father. I still have not regained my memory of the trial. When it was time to be cross-examined, the adversary counsel began to read to me. He read my poetry out loud—poetry that I had written years before and had left in the house when I left with the children. It was sensitive poetry about my hopes and dreams for a beautiful life after the birth of my son Randy. It was about my hopes and dreams of a wondrous marriage.

It was contrary to the life about which I had testified. I must have seemed like a liar. I could not explain the discrepancy. But I did not lie. I remember as I wrote that poetry that it was a dream and not what life was really like. The judge heard the poetry as Sidney's attorney read, then asked, "Did you write this, Ms. C?" My head began to spin and I felt dizzy. He did it to me again. My own words were turned against me. "Yes," I replied, as I sank deeply into the witness chair and tears welled in my eyes. When we had a break for lunch I threw up. I told my attorney I was not going back on the stand. I couldn't. I wouldn't. I don't know or care what he said to the judge. I simply told him I was too sick and he had to do something. He did. I didn't testify again that day.

That day was the first time that I realized I could not articulate what had happened to me. I could not explain to anyone else what my life had been like. I knew I had become swallowed up by him. Our surface life seemed pleasant. We had three beautiful children. I was never injured physically. I remember desperately trying to understand it. After all, if I could not understand it, how could a judge? I was not able to understand or explain it before the judge made a decision. My husband was granted overnight and frequent visitation.

I began to piece my early relationship back together. I felt responsible for what had happened to me and what I knew would happen to my children if I didn't find a way to protect them. During the course of our ten years together, I had lost touch with my feelings. I had become anxious at the thought of an expression of a feeling. He was disappointed that I loved my family. That meant I wasn't independent. He was disappointed that my friends were not well-read. He only liked intellectuals. Of course I never did get his full approval. In the process I dropped my family and friends to please him, and looked only to him for approval. On rare occasions I got partial approval, and that was when I would actually quote something he had said back to him.

I never really came to grips with my family. My mother was tough, strong-willed, and somewhat unyielding in her positions. If I shared information about something or someone with her, she used that same information at a later date in an irrelevant conversation to say or imply something negative about me. Her intent was not evil. Her intent was generally to get me to see her point and to change something. I had learned that behavior, as a child, in the context of being loved.

The difference was that Sidney had used information to try to destroy who I was and to create me into an image of what he wanted me to be. I will never understand it completely. All I know was that

I had to protect my children from him, otherwise he would define their feelings for them. He would label their feelings as he had done mine, as ridiculous or foolish or middle class, all the while making clear his disapproval and disdain.

He would make them feel unhappy with who they were and what they felt. My hope was to let my children learn to trust their own perceptions. But the judge gave him overnight visitation. It seems I did a terrible job testifying. I could not explain why he was so unhealthy for the children. At that time, David was ten years old, Randy was five, and Ramona was two. In my crystal ball I saw my children becoming his victims no matter what I did. I could only try to give them the tools to deal with him.

The next few years are a blur. Visitation was always an ordeal. The kids would come home ravenously hungry. They would be angry with me. Frequently, after a visit they would be violent to me or to each other. I never knew if he fed them or the stress made them hungry or angry. They resisted going and they did not discuss the visit when they returned.

Often, Randy would come home "needing" a new toy. I could just hear Sidney telling him that he had too many toys or that toys were bad, or toys show bad values. Randy found his ways to resist. It wasn't that I thought that Randy or any child should have everything he wanted. Their father was determined to stop the feeling of even wanting. Sidney hated sports. Sidney hated violence. Randy loved wrestling and karate. David found his niche in more intellectual pursuits—the brain of the computer. Ramona was attached to me and hated to go with Sidney.

One day, Sidney became physical with her. Trying to "help" her put on a bathing suit, he was very forceful and his fingers hurt her around her thigh in her vaginal area. She was distraught. She came home upset and crying. This had come on the heels of a separate incident. I told Sidney that he needed to be sensitive to Ramona's private parts and her need for privacy. He scoffed at that. I sought supervised visitation. Reluctantly, the court granted it. Sidney filed numerous motions to the court to have visitation, to increase visitation, to allow vacation visitation, etc. I was perpetually in court battling him. The trial had settled nothing.

There were new motions filed by Sidney. He sought repeat evaluations. He was involved with a father's rights group and he sought an evaluation by a psychologist who had been charged with abusing his own daughter and also convicted of drug and weapons crimes.

Finally the judge was incredulous. Until that point, he had seen me as an over-reactive and over-protective parent. When Sidney told him that he was unconcerned that his daughter was evaluated by a man who had pled guilty to weapons and drug charges, his reaction was open surprise. For the first time, the judge saw that Sidney was more interested in getting what he wanted than how he did it, and that he was unconcerned that his daughter might be harmed.

The judge granted me permission to have Ramona's therapist with her during an evaluation. Ramona was spared. It was a turning point in the litigation. We had been litigating for six years. The court finally began to understand what I had been up against. In some respects, it was at that point that I finally won. I was exhausted. I had lived under a microscope for six years. At last, the court understood.

USING AND CHOOSING EXPERTS

In the law, the simple definition of an expert is any individual who has more than a lay person's knowledge in a particular subject area which is beyond the ordinary ken of the court. In custody and visitation litigation, mental health professionals are the experts most frequently used. There are then two ways mental health professionals are necessary and helpful during custody litigation— as therapists or as evaluators. An evaluator makes psychological assessments of the parties or children and or makes a custody or visitation recommendation based on the best interest of the children. A therapist may be called upon to do therapy for one of the adult parties or the children. This may occur before, during, or after litigation. There are many guidelines of which litigants and experts should be aware. The importance of qualified and experienced experts cannot be underestimated. An attorney must choose the right expert for a particular need during litigation. Critically, the attorney must assert an interest in the experts appointed by the court and raise objections when an expert is appointed who lacks appropriate qualifications. The appointment of an expert by the court is a critical phase in the process. If the court selects an expert without the requisite training, then everything that "expert" concludes cannot really be accurately relied upon. Nonetheless, the court will likely rely upon that person. This point is so critical that if there is an allegation of spousal abuse, it is one of the few areas in which, on an interim basis, an appeal of the appointment of that person may be a smart strategy.

The obvious reason for a parent to use an expert of their own selection would be in part to influence the court on the various issues that may arise. The typical issues that come up range from the effects of the domestic abuse on the children and the spousal victim to the best interest determination as to the custodial parent. However, since there is a known causal connection between spouse abuse and child physical and/or sexual abuse, one must also be prepared to deal with those issues. Sometimes it is wise to have a client evaluated before going to court on these issues to see whether an expert diagnoses a woman as having been battered.

Before using an expert successfully in litigation, it is imperative to know what information the attorney is looking for from the expert. Define the expert's role. It is also essential to know what may be derived that can hurt a case and to be prepared to deal with it. Most states have essentially the same privilege of confidentiality for psychologists and social workers as exists between an attorney and a client. That means that if a person goes to a mental health professional for therapy, there is an expectation that everything said is confidential. But the privilege is not an absolute one.

Confidentiality may be breached when it becomes apparent to the court that the therapist has information pertaining to the child's well-being in the care of a parent. When custody and visitation are legal issues, a parent's mental health may have an impact on his or her ability to appropriately parent the child and the confidential relationship between that parent and his or her therapist may be broken. If a husband admitted to violence against the wife or to the child, the confidential relationship may be set aside.

In order to pierce the confidential relationship, the information must have significant relevance to a parent's ability to parent appropriately. Because custody decisions for the child are being made by someone other than the parent, namely a judge, that judge may want or need to know what a child's therapist knows. He may never understand it or fully agree with it, but a child's therapist can be his or her best ally in court, in part because the therapist's ethical duty is to the child and to the child's welfare. With that in mind, a therapist has a somewhat wide berth when a court seeks therapeutic information. Ordinarily that information is pretty sacrosanct. No one without a patient's permission can open that file. But the court, in its role as super parent (*parens patriae*), gets to decide whether the child's therapy will be kept private or not. Privacy may be critical for emotional healing, but in a case involving domestic violence with a child as a witness or a victim, privacy may need to take a backseat to the therapist's being an advocate in court or to the court for the child's needs. It may be more important for the therapist to open the file. A therapist may accomplish this by their requesting the court to permit him to give information to the court or ask a custodial parent to waive privilege. In some states, privilege attorneys are specially appointed for this purpose. This particular circumstance lends itself to bias by a person outside the court. A child therapist's confidentiality is limited by the parents or the court. Thus, in a legal sense, the child cannot have an expectation of confidentiality. There are many ways this can be important to try to permit. If the court imposes supervised visitation based on a history of violence to the child, the spouse may deny the prior violence. If, during the course of marriage the violence was known to a treating therapist, the information would be important for the court to consider. In some states a parent has a right to use corporal punishment. Further, if the level of violence to the child was considered abuse, the therapist would have had a legal obligation to report it to the local child protection agency. So there may be dilemmas for the therapist.

While confidentiality might be broken, the information may not produce the desired result. It is therefore imperative to know how information will help or hinder the victim's position before suggesting revealing that information to the court. It would not help to suggest to the court that a spouse was violent to the child and that his therapist was aware of the violence, if, when the therapist was requested to give information, the therapist states that the violence was not abusive and that the spouse was perfectly capable of parenting the child.

Therapists are ethically required to protect the best interest of their clients. If during the course of treatment spousal abuse was acknowledged to the therapist, and a therapist could testify that the husband has a problem controlling anger or violence to the victim, this may be helpful. Knowing the parameters for revealing information and how it can be used in the particular circumstance can guide whether and when to seek to open this door or to attempt to keep privilege.

The attorney should inquire as to the therapist's position and understanding of what has happened before the therapist reports to the court. It is up to the attorney to ensure that the information is actually used to the benefit of the victim or the child.

There are concerns when battered women face information, if known about them or their personal history, will be detrimental to a case for custody. One obvious example is a problem with drug use or alcohol for which treatment has been sought.

During the course of litigation, one must assume that an abuser will accuse the victim of manipulating or brainwashing the children. In general, the assumption should be made that the abuser will find a way to use everything negative about the victim to his advantage. Sometimes the information will be used to obfuscate issues; sometimes it will be used to deflect issues. For many abusers, the goal of a custody case is not for custody. It is not to best meet the needs of the children. Their goal is to find a way to further control the victim. In court, the best way to continue to hurt a battered spouse is through the threat of removal of the children from her custody through the court system.

An expert is often necessary to explain what appear to be inconsistent behaviors. For example, a woman may have used corporal punishment on her children. She expresses fear her husband will hurt the children, but she knows that she, too, has been guilty of what will be considered harsh treatment of her children. An expert on domestic abuse will take the woman's own history and make an assessment of her likelihood to harm the child, or to stop hurting the child once the victim is no longer at risk from abuse. The woman may have been a victim of parental abuse or simply so battered that she took her own frustration out on the children. In either case, an expert in spousal abuse can put her behavior into a perspective that can be understood by the court. Thus, if the husband testifies to the wife's harsh treatment, this behavior has already been adequately addressed so as to minimize its effect on the litigation. Indeed, abused women may use more severe means of punishment on their children when they are being victimized by their spouses. When no longer a victim, the battered spouse decreases these more severe forms of punishment on her children. Thus, if the wife has been in therapy during the marriage and acknowledges hitting her children, her own therapist may be called upon to provide this information. It is important to plan in advance of being confronted. Again, this is important and must be dealt with in pleadings. However, an expert in the area of spousal abuse is important here because genuine concerns for the welfare of a child must be dealt with by the court. An explanation will help the court understand and mitigate concerns about children in the wife's custody.

Frequently, courts appoint a mental health professional to do a best interest evaluation. The stated purpose of the evaluation is to assist the court in meeting the child's custodial and relationship needs with both parents. One of the most difficult things to do is combat an adverse court-appointed evaluation. For this reason it is imperative that the attorney participate in the process of appointing an evaluator. Where the court chooses an individual without input from attorneys, the attorney must voice concerns about the chosen professional in advance of the evaluation. If someone without the requisite training is appointed, it is a concern worth appealing. Admittedly, this is a time-consuming and costly tactic. It is necessary because once an adverse report is issued by a mental health professional who the judge trusts and respects, the only likely way to combat the report's recommendations is to choose, at the victim's financial expense, a different evaluator.

Furthermore, the trustworthiness of the evaluator hired by the victim, an interested party, will of course be suspect. Court rules do not generally permit the judge to give more weight to one expert than another during the pendency of a case. Nevertheless, it is up to a court to assess credibility and weight of the evidence during a trial.

In addition, most litigants cannot afford to do an appeal during the pendency of litigation due to their high cost. Judges know this. They therefore do things that probably could or would be overturned on appeal were they judged to be held accountable to a higher court. For example, I was forced to bring an emergent matter to the court's attention based on a report by an expert evaluator who believed two young children were at risk of harm in the father's unsupervised care. The previous judge had ordered the father's girlfriend to supervise visitation. The evaluator felt that it was not sufficient to protect the children's needs. The court, as it entered an order, indicated that the court appointed evaluator disagreed with my client's expert (an acknowledged nationally known expert) and the court felt the court appointed evaluator was clearly unbiased. Further, the judge articulated his belief that it was "terrible" that my client had taken her two children out of state for an evaluation. The judge never mentioned concern for the welfare of the children as a result of what the evaluator said. It didn't concern the court that this was done in an effort to try to protect the children. Despite the fact that it is absolutely against court rules in that state to give more weight to the court expert, this judge did so and even stated it. Further, the children's emotional state was ignored, although a renowned expert on violence felt the children were at risk. The judge, however, articulated his position that it was terrible for the children that the children were taken by the mother out of state. How could the judge not understand this mother's need to try to protect her children and to do everything possible to make the court understand what her children needed for protection? Just because the renowned expert in violence did not happen to be in New Jersey, should the court ignore the violence and the children's pleas for protection? Despite a documented history of serious violence for eight years and undocumented violence even before that, the court chose not to listen to the renowned expert.

What are the criteria to choose an expert as an evaluator in a domestic abuse case? First, the individual should be is a licensed mental health professional with professional ethical guidelines. Second, the attorney must ascertain the critical issues for the case. The expert in any domestic abuse case must have expertise in domestic abuse. He or she must know the effects of domestic abuse on women and on children and be able to differentiate between an appropriately concerned victim from a psychologically unhealthy parent.

The expert must have experience as a forensic evaluator in the area of domestic abuse. Knowledge without experience and without training is not enough. One therefore must explore what training and experience the expert has. Frequently, women who work at battered women's shelters will know. There are now credentialing organizations in domestic abuse. The attorney should personally call the proposed experts, ask hypothetical questions, and listen carefully to the answers. If the proposed expert does not appear to have sufficient knowledge, expertise, or experience, the attorney should strenuously object to the person being appointed. Attorneys should inquire about testing procedures and information the proposed expert will rely on to make determinations. How will the proposed expert assess information about prior violence if none exists at this time? How does the expert believe children are affected by early violence in the home even though they have not been direct victims?

The answers should provide the attorney with sufficient information to make a judgment about the expert's fund of knowledge and expertise. The attorney must have knowledge of the problems and explore that with any potential expert. This is the most difficult area. The attorney must be comfortable with his or her own knowledge in the area of domestic abuse. If an attorney is not sufficiently knowledgeable in the domestic field, he or she should not take a domestic abuse case.

The importance of choosing the right expert both individually and by the court cannot be overemphasized. An expert does not have to agree with every aspect of a case. Most important is that the expert has the requisite knowledge to correctly perform the assessment. If the "expert" is not truly an expert in the area they will opine, the correct determination cannot be made. If an inadequate expert is selected, a correct determination is pure guesswork. It is then more likely that more litigation will be created by the need to collaterally attack the expert. done.

In like manner, if the abuser is dissatisfied with the report of the evaluator, he will also have the right to choose an expert. It does not stop litigation to choose a good expert. However, it can accomplish certain goals. If an expert is chosen with care and does an appropriate job, the abuser choosing his own expert will have less impact on the litigation. In our experience, once the domestic abuse is overlooked by an evaluator, it is extremely difficult to get the court to understand the importance of the impact of domestic abuse. If the violence is appropriately evaluated and its impact correctly assessed by an evaluator, the court has a context from which to assess problems that may arise with the children during the course of litigation.

The court will usually not modify interim orders based solely on an expert evaluation. However, it lays the foundation for problems as they arise. The evaluation will also set the stage for the evaluator chosen by the husband. That is to say, if the expert is lacking expertise, cross-examination will be very revealing. If the husband's chosen expert has real expertise and the woman is really battered, the expert will acknowledge the battering and it will be difficult to explain away why the victim of abuse is not the better parent.

The expert initially chosen by the court will also have been able to explain problems the children may be having as a result of having lived with an abusive parent, even if they have not been themselves victims of physical violence. Their emotional turmoil will be understood. Further, the expert can explain personality characteristics of the abuser and make predictions about the children in his care.

Sometimes after an evaluation is complete, therapy is recommended for the children or one or both spouses. The therapist who works with children is often their best ally in court. The therapist has one critical concern—the good mental health of his or her patient. The therapist can have no allegiance to either parent. Therefore, especially where there has been a good evaluation, a good therapist is important in the process of litigating and protecting children. If the therapist is unsophisticated on the issue of violence, he or she may present alternative reasons for behaviors to the court inconsistent with the prior violence. Therefore, the choice of therapist in this circumstance is equally critical as choice of an expert, and it should be done with similar care and concern. Furthermore, one would not want an unsophisticated therapist to treat a child.

In sum, experts must be carefully screened and selected. They must be used to establish and strengthen a position. They give credence to the need for change in visitation schedules and other matters involving a child's best interests. Too many attorneys leave the expert selection process to chance or they assume that all experts are equal. In domestic abuse, to leave it to chance or assume equality is to effectively ignore the client's interests. The expert chosen by a court for evaluation or therapy may mean the difference between the custody in favor of the victim or the abuser. The correct use of experts takes time and money. This must be explained to the client so that within the framework of financial feasibility the best choices are made.

[10]

DEVELOPING STRATEGIES

The most difficult part of a domestic abuse law practice is developing strategies on behalf of the battered wife and then carrying them out. The most insurmountable problems occur in domestic abuse custody cases because there is no strategy, and the attorney is being reactive rather than proactive. A plan is essential to success. Working with the battered spouse complicates this difficult task. The nature of the custody case, the attendant high cost of litigation, and a system that perpetuates the great judicial fallacy, all add tremendous stress.

An attorney cannot guarantee a successful outcome, no matter how much money is spent. The experience of being battered by someone who claims to have loved you causes a victim to have difficulty in trusting relationships. The high cost and slow process of litigation add to the distrust. In the process of carrying out a strategy, communication is key and the battered spouse must participate actively in the process and understand and make the decisions for herself and her children's best interests.

To create the strategy and to gain the trust of the battered spouse minimally requires two things. First, the strategy must make sense, be understood, and agreed upon by the victim.

Second, communication must remain open and clear between the attorney and the client.

Before an attorney can work successfully with a victim, the attorney must appreciate the difficulty of working with someone who is in the midst of extricating herself from a battering relationship. The battered woman's fear is not gone just because she has left the batterer. Violence often escalates upon leaving. The woman will know the risks to her and her children best. Fear will pervade the entire course of litigation and may have an adverse impact on the attorney's ability to help her protect her children. She may want to appease the batterer. Appeasement does not work. If she desires to modify the strategy at some point, the attorney must ask the victim if this is appeasement or her best judgment for the children's best interest. Refocusing is a constant. Jointly, the attorney and victim may decide to compromise, but the compromise should be made from knowledge and not from fear.

Each issue that arises during litigation may require numerous and repetitive discussions. What seems simple to the attorney may be overwhelming to the victim. She may not articulate her fears, concerns, or even her thoughts. While she may not emotionally trust, she may, in fact, give undue reliance on her attorney. The attorney must ask questions, elicit the victim's concerns and thoughts, and together decide the best way to proceed. This process makes carrying out a strategy difficult and time consuming, but it keeps the communication open and the victim involved in making decisions.

Too often victims choose lawyers who do not have an understanding of domestic abuse and who do not plan a strategy accordingly. When that happens, the victim winds up changing lawyers, sometimes two or three times, before finding someone with whom she is compatible. By that time, the victim may be even more demanding and be less trusting. The case may have gone from bad to worse and the victim may have failed to protect her children.

It is accepted that when one goes to a doctor, there may be stress and the doctor may be in a hurry. For these reasons, one is often advised to prepare a list of questions before going so one does not forget them. Likewise, it is wise for litigants to create such a list before meeting with potential new counsel. Mental health professionals can assist in the initial question and follow-up questions. It is important to spend time reflecting on the answers after the appointment as well. The mental health professional can do that with a client and perhaps create additional questions before the attorney is hired. Sometimes the mental health professional can even assist in a telephone interview.

When a case is taken over from another attorney, the new attorney must read the entire file to know what has transpired so that an effective strategy can be developed. Undertaking representation of a battered woman in the middle of litigation without a strategy simply fosters the continuation of a downhill spiral. The first step in developing a mid-course strategy is to understand what transpired up to the point the new attorney entered the case. To know what has already occurred requires knowledge of the written pleadings filed in the case, the transcripts of court appearances that are available, and correspondence and expert reports.

From the written pleadings, the attorney learns what has and has not been said. All reports and court orders should be read to assess what impressions the court has of the client and of the adversary, as well as what the court believes is currently appropriate to meet the child's best interests. The new attorney must also ascertain what problems the client has to overcome in order to meet her burden of proof.

A strategy must be reasonable given the particular set of circumstances. The first step is to understand the detailed facts of the case which have been presented to the court. The attorney must also comprehend the detailed facts presented by the history the client has either given to the attorney verbally or in writing. Which specific parts of the court record have been inaccurately understood by the court? It is important to ascertain what actual proofs may exist by way of witnesses, police or hospital reports, phone records, and other evidence to corroborate the client's descriptions of events.

It is a good idea for the attorney to create an outline list of problems and what must be done to address them, including a list of inaccuracies stated by the adversary. Which proofs can show lies, misstatements, or twists of truth or fact? Where there are no proofs, a detailed knowledge from the client of what actually occurred is essential. Court impressions come from pleadings, court behavior, or expert opinion.

The pleadings previously prepared by a predecessor counsel need to be carefully examined. Any new attorney should identify relevant information that is hoped will persuade the court to the client's perspective of what is needed to preserve the children's best interests. Theoretically, no case is won or lost until a decision is issued after a trial. In reality, judges are human and have propensities in handling cases. For this reason, the strategy that is developed pre-trial is designed to get the correct impression to the court before the trial. Seeds must be sown during pretrial litigation. Questions and concerns must be appropriately raised on all issues as they arise. The court then has time to integrate those issues and concerns to its thinking. Then, upon proofs at trial—if the matter does not settle beforehand—there is a hope of changing the court's perspective.

Well thought-out strategies that are devised and implemented at the outset yield the best chance of prevailing during litigation. Parenthetically, if a solid strategy is developed and followed and is successful at pre-trial, the abuser may see that it is to his advantage to settle the case.

When the pleadings of the predecessor counsel are read, a new attorney should attempt to go back in time to a position of neutrality and read them with fresh eyes. Did the woman overreact? Did she appear hysterical or overly concerned? What was missing from the pleadings to persuade a court she was right? Is there information that, had it been provided logically, would have modified the court's perception and ruling? The key here is simply to apply what we know about human nature, about creating an impression and/ or changing an impression, to make an assessment.

Another part of developing a strategy is implementation. Implementation involves contingency plans and alternative strategies and re-assessments throughout the course of litigation. Looking at the case with a critical eye is a process that must be repeated throughout the litigation. A reasonable estimate of what can be accomplished and what is necessary to achieve the desired reasonable result must be carried out during the preparation of pleadings, expert evaluations, therapy, therapy reports, and other opportunities to have an impact on the court.

For instance, an attorney enters a case in which there is acknowledged domestic abuse. The court entered a restraining order after finding that domestic abuse occurred. Then a divorce proceeding commenced. A motion was submitted by the wife seeking support and for entry of visitation orders. No history of the violence was described. The restraining order prohibited curbside drop-off and pick-up of children.

No one had requested that the parties could not confer as to the children and the court permitted such contact by telephone. Litigation proceeded, but then visitation conflicts arose. The wife filed motions seeking to restrict the husband from calling her. She complained that her husband is calling her at home in a harassing fashion. She may or may not have filed violations of the restraining order complaints. An expert evaluation by a court appointed person ensued. Perhaps the expert was not specifically credentialed in the area of domestic abuse. The custody report found the mother to be the appropriate custodial parent, but found no problem for the parents to have joint custody and joint conferring on major decisions of the children's lives. The wife reported the violence to the expert and conveyed to the expert that she was having difficulty in resolving anything with her husband. Nevertheless, there is no or little discussion about the violence in the report.

What does an attorney do when he or she enters the case, reviews the file, and sees that there has been liberal visitation, pleadings that have not outlined in any great detail a history of violence, an expert report that identifies no problems with the abuser having joint custody and a lot of time with the children, and a client who says there are significant problems for the children with the current arrangement? There are no motions pending and the children are not in therapy. The new attorney must have new information to present. In the aforementioned case, the court has already rejected the client's reasoning. The evaluator also sees no need for change. To seek a change without new information would be to give the court bad impressions about the client and perhaps make her look unreasonable. The best strategy would be to seek advice of another expert, one who is truly knowledgeable in the area of domestic abuse.

How does an attorney know if an independent evaluation is necessary? In choosing that route, the best scenario an attorney may achieve is an expert who will contradict the findings of the other evaluator. It may be a better strategy instead to make certain the child is in good therapy. Another evaluation can be obtained later, and that option can be reserved. It is better to have a good child assessment and later, if necessary, seek a new court-appointed custody evaluation from someone who is appropriately credentialed. Or even if the initial person who conducted the custody evaluation is called back to do an update, in light of a therapist' s concerns, that evaluator will now have to consider the needs of a child through the eyes of the expert who has the ethical responsibility of protecting the mental health of the child.

Although therapy is not an evaluation, all therapy involves an initial assessment of a problem. The wife should bring the child. The presenting problem is whatever problems the wife describes or, if the child is old enough, the problem as described by the child. The therapist gets to know the child and a rapport develops. It is hoped that the etiology of the child's concerns will also be learned. In any case, the domestic abuse ramifications can and should be dealt with as a part of therapy.

During the course of therapy, if the therapist feels that the evaluator was correct as to the child's benefitting from more time with the father, the wife's attorney now has that knowledge to build on and can prepare future strategy accordingly. If the therapist agrees that change in visitation is necessary, then the choice is to either have an evaluation conducted on behalf of the client or go back to court. It is likely that the attorney would go back to court.

How does an attorney prepare to request a modification from the court when modification in visitation has already been refused by a prior application? The request must be accompanied minimally by two things. First, the attorney should have the therapist's opinion, in writing, that a modification is necessary for the mental health of the child, and the therapist must state the basis for this determination. It would also be helpful if the therapist can explain why his or her opinion differs from the evaluator's.

Second, a certification or affidavit or declaration (a sworn to statement) from the client is required. The need to go to court provides the attorney with the opportunity to provide the missing history to the court about the history of domestic abuse. Using the procedural history method of writing the events raises questions about the evaluator's initial evaluation. The attorney may want to raise the issue of a new evaluation. Strategically however, it may be better to just plant the seed in a certification and request a modification that the therapist feels is necessary for the child. When domestic abuse is alleged, custody becomes a power battle for the abuser and a battle of child protection for the wife. The case cannot be about what the wife wants. The focus must always be on what the court feels is necessary for the child.

Assuming the motion for modification is granted, the attorney has accomplished two goals. Some measure of credibility has been gained in the eyes of the court for the need for modification, and there been success in helping the child on behalf of the mother.

Once again, it is time to strategize. The case is not over. It is difficult to plan precisely, but the attorney should always be strategizing. Based on what the batterer will do next, based on the responses he gave to the request for relief, what does the wife's attorney do next? If settlement is possible it should always be explored.

Assuming settlement is not possible, and relief has been granted, then the child must continue in therapy. It is important to mention that the period necessary before a therapist may be able to express that opinion will vary. This scenario also presumes that the child was not in immediate danger. In the event the parent believes there is immediate danger, an assessment of that danger must be presented to an evaluator. In this case, the evaluation would not be one of best interest. It would be a mental status evaluation to assess immediate and/or emergent mental health needs for the child. In this scenario, a therapist may be simultaneously engaged to get the therapist role established. An attorney does not want to have to litigate the choosing of a therapist in court while the child does not get necessary therapy. Also, if the court does not recognize the need for special knowledge, it may appoint someone not competent in this area who may then rubber stamp the evaluator, merely out of lack of knowledge of the impact of domestic abuse. Thus, to the extent possible, the attorney wants to try to exercise control in selection of experts competent in the field of domestic abuse.

Frequently, at this juncture, the therapist comes under attack by the abuser. The attorney should be prepared with another expert to back up the theories propounded by the therapist. In either case the therapeutic relationship is a critical one for the child and may, over time, be the one relied upon by the court. If the therapist comes under attack, it is simply something that is going to have to be dealt with. Most therapists will contact both parents. This will depend on the custody and ethical responsibilities, as seen by the individual. The ramifications of doing it either way should be explored by the attorney in advance to help protect the integrity of the therapist.

Once a therapeutic relationship is established, it is generally thought to be more adverse to a child's mental health to disrupt that relationship. Therefore, many judges will not interfere with that relationship. If it becomes clear that the attorney must get another evaluation, the attorney should try first to get another court-appointed individual with the necessary domestic abuse background and make sure the appointment allows the attorney to provide necessary materials to the evaluator.

It is likely that the adversary will argue for an update rather than a new evaluator, if he or she likes the evaluation. Assuming that happens, the best strategy is to let the court know the detailed problems with the current evaluator's lack of knowledge and expertise. If the report is critically dealt with by the wife's attorney or another expert, there is a chance to prevail. In the worst case scenario, the wife's attorney will be forced to get an evaluator on the wife's behalf.

At each stage during the course of the litigation, there may be other issues with which the attorney needs to deal. As we have previously mentioned, the battered woman may be a difficult client. At times, she may even appear irrational. Her attorney may wonder if all the things the adversary client says about her are really true. The victim may need an inordinate amount of time for reassurance and explanation. She may change her mind frequently. She may forget. She may say she forgot something you believed was clear. She is supposed to let you know about problems with visitation, as they arise. Instead, she says nothing and then you get a letter from her adversary's attorney complaining about the problems she is causing. The wife's attorney discusses the matter with the victim and explains the importance of keeping the attorney apprised. She agrees to do so next time. She doesn't. The attorney becomes frustrated.

Most attorneys are taught to be reactive. Representation where there is abuse on a spouse needs proactive representation. One needs to know the potential outcomes and to carry the strategy with the use of experts and education of the court to logical conclusions.

Frequently, judges are called upon to make interim custodial and visitation decisions. While the term "interim" may suggest a temporary solution, the ruling could be in effect for several years and have lasting effects on children and their families. A temporary decision by a judge may even provide avenues through which family violence continues.

There are tools that can help the court remain child centered and sensitive to abuse issues in a child custody case. A lawyer must understand these tools in order to form a strategy for protecting children during the course of custody and visitation litigation. While there are many ways to educate the court and to favorably position one's case prior to trial, the impact of the abuse upon the child is the filter through which all information should be presented. The strategies that we suggest are designed to keep the court focused on the needs and welfare of the child. Further, employing the strategy of using permissible motions and hearings also helps keep the court from using a criminal standard (which requires an overarching concern for the rights of the defendant and securing the rights of the accused) rather than promoting the welfare of the child.

In the early stages of a case, the court should apply what is known from the literature about the effects of domestic abuse on children. Children are at risk when they are exposed to one parent controlling the other by power, coercion, exploitation, put downs, threats, and/or physical or sexual violence. When the court ignores this abuse in making visitation orders, child safety takes a back seat to parental rights. Without a showing of risk of harm to a child, it is difficult to reduce contact between a parent and their child because of the understanding under the U.S. Constitution that adults have the right to parent their children.

A judge who lacks information about family violence is likely to consider due process and what would appear to be fair for each parent. However, recognition of the due process rights of the parents does not guarantee protection for a child. A problem occurs when a child is a direct victim of, a witness of, or has been exposed to abuse. The court should question what can be done to keep a child emotionally and physically safe, help a child recover from their trauma, and prevent re-traumatization. A court order that reduces or eliminates contact between the abuser and the child may not alone produce the desired effect. In many cases, without treatment, the child's fear of abuse does not end. Untreated trauma may result in behavioral problems and ultimately in psychopathology and, thus, the child remains unprotected. This scenario may send the wrong messages to the child and the abusive parent. The child comes to believe that their parents, professionals, and the courts will not protect them. At the same time, the abusive parent may think that the court will allow parental rights to take precedence. The stage is then set for the abusive parent to continue to victimize during the litigation, leaving the child at risk.

The use of a variety of pretrial strategies helps remind the court about the abuse and may help keep the court more focused on the child's rights rather than abusive parent's rights. In practice, crucial information is often lost or is given little weight by the court because evidence of abuse has not been presented in detail either by the victim or counsel. I have found this to be true even in cases in which there have been findings of fact that validate the allegations of abuse resulting in domestic abuse restraining orders.

Attorneys who wait until a custody or visitation trial to present evidence of abuse potentially squander invaluable opportunities to educate the court, argue their client's position early, create a record, and perhaps exclude or limit spurious defenses and/or testimony from proposed experts. Various strategies can be used during pretrial hearings, including focusing attention on the sufficiency of scientific/medical/psychological certainty concerning proposed expert testimony; factors affecting reliability of child testimony; access to historical and current information about the parties (e.g., personnel records); and the qualifications and appointments of particular experts, Guardians ad Litem, and/or evaluators.

Tort claims. Tort claims (i.e., suits for damages) are valid and important litigation remedies. These actions are not based on a contract and are referred to in the law as a tort. When a marriage partner injures the other partner during the marriage, there may be a cause of action in the court for damages sustained as a result of the injuries. These injuries are sometimes physical, as with assault and battery, and sometimes emotional, such as with battered women's syndrome and posttraumatic stress disorder. A tort complaint sets forth a detailed history of abuse and serves as a road map for the court to better understand the history of the parties' relationship. The complaint can be filed on behalf of a party or on behalf of children who have sustained damages as a result of injury by a parent. These claims require support by an expert.

In certain circumstances, these actions are joined with and may later be separated from the divorce action. A separate tort claim allows for the possibility of a jury trial, which affords an opportunity to explain to the court the behavior of the abusing spouse as well as its effect on the children. Whether a tort claim remains a part of the divorce action or not, the claim itself, where valid, provides an opportunity to review matters of abuse in the family that might otherwise be glossed over in a divorce action.

Pretrial hearings. Another strategy that may be helpful is for a party to file a motion seeking a pretrial ruling on whether the opposing side's expert is qualified and using reliable data, and whether the expert's opinion is consistent with the standard of practice. Courts may be reluctant to hold pretrial admissibility hearings in custody matters, believing that psychologists and social workers rely on accepted studies, methods, or practices. It is worth pursuing in order to alert the court that the adversary's position is weak by exposing and undermining the opposing expert if he or she relied on suspect procedures, articles, studies, or junk science. It alerts the opposing counsel that experts are going to be held to high professional standards. It is also an opportunity to explain to the court the impact of violence on the child as well as a reemphasis on the importance of relying upon qualified experts. This may prevent the judge from agreeing with an attack on the expert and bolster the court's faith in testimony by the person who presents the victim's point of view.

An attack on the other side's expert early in the process may set the tone for the eventual trial, and it may help focus the court on the child's welfare. In all family law cases, attorneys must assist the court to maintain its focus on issues related to the risk of physical as well as emotional harm to the child. In New Jersey, criminal procedures through the Rules of Court allow for pretrial hearings about particular evidentiary issues. States commonly set forth a framework in criminal practice to deal with some evidentiary issues pretrial. There are hearings to resolve issues relating to the admissibility of statements by a defendant, pretrial identifications of defendant, sound recordings, and motions to suppress evidence. There is a substantially identical rule for municipal matters in New Jersey. Curiously, in New Jersey, civil practice does not have a similar rule. Family courts, in particular, have been reluctant to apply a similar framework to flush out and resolve issues in advance of a trial. The Rules of Evidence, unlike the Rules of Court, however, provide some guidelines regarding the use of pretrial hearings as a means of resolving admissibility issues.

Each state adopts its own Rules of Evidence. Some state rules conform to the federal rules, while others do not. While each state rule may differ slightly, there is a broad similarity overall. For expert testimony to be admissible under New Jersey Rule of Evidence 702, the discipline, methodology, or premises relied upon by the expert must be sufficiently reliable. The issue of admissibility of expert testimony is whether the experts' methods and premises are "generally accepted" under the *Frye* standard. "The court's role is to 'determine whether the expert's opinion is derived from a sound and well-founded methodology that is supported by some expert consensus in the appropriate field" (*Landrigan v. Celotex Corp.*, 1992, p. 417). The parties have a right to challenge the expert's methodology and to challenge the reliability of any findings based upon that methodology in an evidentiary hearing, the purpose of which is to demonstrate that the testimony is so lacking in foundation as to be worthless. The court should hold an evidentiary hearing pursuant to New Jersey Rule of Evidence 104 to determine the admissibility of challenged evidence. Judges are gatekeepers for determining whether proffered evidence and its consistency and compliance with an underlying theory of science and scientifically based methods of assessment meet the criteria for admissible scientific evidence. There are two major cases that assist courts in making that determination. Some states use Frye, some use Daubert, and others use a combination of the two cases.

The judge's task under *Frye* is relatively simple: to determine whether the method employed by the experts is generally accepted in the scientific community. Under *Daubert v. Merrill Dow Pharmaceuticals, Inc.*, there is a difficult two-part analysis. First, it must be determined whether the experts' testimony reflects "scientific knowledge," whether their findings are "derived by the scientific method," and whether their work product amounts to "good science." Second, the court must ensure that the proposed expert testimony is "relevant to the task at hand" (i.e., that it logically advances a material aspect of the proposing party's case).

"The *Daubert* case was returned to the 9th Circuit Court and again, the scientific evidence proffered by the plaintiffs was rejected by the Court *Daubert v. Merrell Dow Pharmaceuticals, Inc. (on remand)*, 43 F.3d. 1311 [9th Cir. 1995]). Judge Alex Kozinski, writing for the Court, declared that '[s]omething doesn't become 'scientific knowledge' just because it's uttered by the scientist. . .' (at 1315–16). The Court's task, Kozinski wrote, 'is to analyze not what the experts say, but what basis they have for saying it'" (at 1316). Most states have adopted The Federal Evidence Rule 702 for the admissibility of forensic expert testimony The rule provides

A witness who is qualified as an expert by knowledge, skill, experience, training, or education may testify in the form of an opinion or otherwise if

(a) the expert's scientific, technical, or other specialized knowledge will help the trier of fact to understand the evidence or to determine a fact in issue;

(b) the testimony is based on sufficient facts or data;

(c) the testimony is the product of reliable principles and methods; and

(d) the expert has reliably applied the principles and methods to the facts of the case.

Rule 702 has been adopted by a majority of states. As can be seen, to the extent Rule 702 may not be adopted, then the general rules of Frye and Daubert are the rules governing admissibility.

While the *Daubert* court clarified for federal courts that the standard for expert testimony lies in the federal Rules of Evidence, not all states have adopted the more stringent Daubert standards. However, both the Frye and the Daubert standards represent the basis upon which courts determine the admissibility of challenged testimony. After *Frye* or *Daubert* hearings, the court is left with testimony that is more reliable. Due process requires an equal opportunity to present qualified experts, not necessarily the same number for both sides.

The other party's employment or personnel records, police reports, or medical or psychological records may be relevant to the allegations asserted in a custody action. Such information may provide direct evidence on the issues at question and may be subpoenaed. In addition, as a part of a thorough custody evaluation, evaluators can seek to obtain this collateral data from current and historical records where abuse is an issue.

A party may seek to keep these records from being disclosed by asserting a privacy right. In that event, an opportunity presents itself for filing a brief and requesting a hearing. In many cases, the information sought may provide "other bad acts" or damaging information that the court should weigh in its final and ultimate custody determination. Even if the court ultimately keeps the information from being disclosed, the facts and circumstances of the information will have been made known to the court. In family matters, the rules often are not strictly adhered to, so information that might otherwise be kept from view of the court may be considered relevant to the best interests of a child. Of course, if the information is deemed impermissible, the court is not permitted to place any reliance upon it in making a final determination.

Often a party's expert(s) will testify about the child's statements to the expert or to other investigators. The data from these interviews are considered hearsay, though experts may be permitted to testify about hearsay evidence in certain circumstances; for example, if it is the type of information normally relied upon by an expert conducting such an evaluation. Typically the expert will present a written report that may contain statements made by a child. Also, the expert may be asked to testify as to the same statements that were in the written report. In some states and in certain circumstances, expert reports may be admissible. Absent consent by both parties or unless the written report is a statement subject to one of the hearsay exceptions, it can generally be kept from being admitted as evidence for consideration and only the testimony of the expert will be considered as evidence at trial.

Experts may present to the court statements and interpretations that conflict with those provided by a child. The expert is often permitted to testify as to the child's statements because they are considered information or facts normally relied upon by experts in that field. Cross-examining the adversary's expert as to the child's purported statements can be made more difficult if the child's statements are not recorded. Even when they are recorded, the expert's questions, demeanor, technique, body language, and timing can greatly affect whether the child will talk about the relevant issues and whether the child will feel comfortable enough to divulge sometimes stressful information to a stranger (Patel & Choate, 2014).

Sometimes courts interview children. Such interviews may be mandatory unless doing so would harm the child. An attorney may seek to have a child interviewed by the court. There may be a hearing to determine whether there will also be testimony by a child in court or out of court and/or by videotape. If an interview is videotaped by the court, there is an opportunity to view the child's statements in a different light and to review them as many times as necessary. Another strategy is to challenge the competency of the child to testify. A competency hearing provides the opportunity to put issues of concern for the child's welfare before the court.

Independent party-selected versus court-appointed evaluators. When the issue of custody and visitation is presented, there is a question about whether to rely upon an independent, party-selected expert or a court-appointed expert. Part of a judge's task lies in understanding the expertise, neutrality, and bias of evaluators. Sometimes judges rule out appointing the very experts they ought to be choosing because that expert "finds" more child abuse. Just because someone works in the field of domestic abuse and child abuse does not make that person inherently biased and does not mean that person believes that everyone is a domestic abuse perpetrator or child abuser. Proper training and experience makes them credentialed.

Before an evaluation is conducted, sometimes it is helpful to file a motion challenging the adequacy of a court-appointed evaluator's credentials. Abuse victims are more likely to select a mental health professional who is an expert in abuse-related issues just as a medical patient would see a cardiovascular surgeon for heart surgery and not go to a general surgeon. If a child remains fearful because of her father's past violence, would she heal best if forced to visit her father? Can you imagine ever telling a child who had seen a street fight that the most violent person in the fight would babysit them that night? An attorney must bring these concerns to the judge by filing motions.

A professional's report on the status of the child who was emotionally hurt by family violence should be part of the information brought before the court at the earliest opportunity. This can take the form of a child abuse evaluation or an assessment to see if a child needs therapy. This type of evaluation would be tantamount to giving a child necessary medical attention. For example, if a child had a broken bone, a parent would not decide if it was broken, nor would she be expected to set the bone. An experienced professional needs to conduct the abuse assessment and make recommendations to the court that result in the child getting proper care. Neither the attorney nor the parent, nor even the court on its own would "set a bone." Likewise, they would not, by themselves, render treatment to an abused child. If therapy is recommended for the child, it should begin immediately unless there is a legal reason it is impermissible. As a case moves forward, it is important that the record reflects that a parent did what one would expect of a parent and not that the parent was simply preparing for litigation. Since most people use doctors to diagnose illnesses, one should do no less in situations involving abuse.

An attorney should be graphic. Convey the degree of fear a person might experience if they were in a serious car accident. The same level of fear may afflict an abused child. Using analogies such as a car accident will most likely enhance the court's understanding of child abuse. For example, traumatic memory may not be recovered as immediately as the memory of a football game on TV. After such an event, most of us recognize that sometimes we cannot remember the details of what happened. Details may come back slowly, unlike the precise mental images that we retain from last night's football game. Furthermore, if a child does not feel safe, she or he may not remember what they witnessed or experienced. Children are vulnerable and need the assurance that when they talk about what happened, they will be believed.

In order to provide maximum protection to abused children, the protective parent or counsel must avail themselves of all of the tools at their disposal from the very start of litigation. Through the use of these and other pretrial procedures and hearings and a thorough presentation of the abuse, the judge will be better educated and the children will be more likely to receive the necessary protection.

[11]

FAMILY COURTS MUST DEMAND SCIENCE

Family courts have the power to keep parents who harm their own children from parenting those children. Indeed, the family court is supposed to weigh in favor of child protection even over the right to parent. The judge is required to act *parens patriae,* essentially as the child's super parent. When cases are presented in court, rules and statutes require that expert testimony, upon which the judge will rely, be reliable and scientifically based.

The sad situation is that despite these requirements and the available remedies for protection, states fail the test of assuring that experts testify based upon what is accepted practice within the scientific community when they are in family court. As a result, aggressive protection of children is bypassed and children are too often placed in harm's way.

The science of child abuse is permitted to be ignored because many judges are not even properly trained to know when there is objectionable unscientific testimony. Lawyers are not required to promote science or have unscientific testimony precluded. Many, if not most, states permit a relaxation of rules for children's best interests, which allows—indeed almost asks for—unscientific testimony and the permitting of speculation by experts rather than the presentation of science. Often orders are entered, long before trials, that do not protect children and are based upon judges' perceptions of facts as opposed to having testimony taken from knowledgeable professionals.

When testimony is taken at an early stage, family courts may permit testimony from unqualified and improperly trained or untrained experts. Too often these individuals promote unacceptable/unscientific practices and demand proofs of abuse that may be impossible to obtain and/or are not scientifically necessary to affirm abuse.

We must begin to demand science from our experts in family courts. Testing and clinical data must be accepted within the family court and be reproducible in accord with accepted practice in the scientific community. Clinical judgments and overall recommendations must be based upon accepted practice in the community that is well versed in the science of abuse.

Family courts are affected by what is commonly accepted in society. There is an inherent disbelief in society as to children's reliability as reporters. It seems to be assumed that children overstate things that happen to them. This social belief contradicts the vast amount of research that says that children do not generally lie about abuse.

Judges and many others too frequently automatically suspect the veracity of children who report abuse, especially when the named abuser is a parent and most especially where the parents are in the middle of divorce. Yet it is common for children to report abuse in a circumstance where they feel safe and protected. So it follows that this would occur on the heels of a parental separation. Yet when a newly separated parent reports a child's disclosure of abuse, the focus of a family court investigation tends to gravitate to an inquisition of the reporting parent's motives, reactions, and feelings rather than a child-focused protective response. This is in itself unscientific.

When the issue of abuse goes to family court, these and other risks predominate. The abuse takes a back seat to the attack on the person who brought it to a court's attention. If this information went instead to a criminal court, the trained investigators and prosecutors have no alternate investigation or evaluation except that of the child. Thus, criminal prosecution demands science. Family court must demand science as well.

Sadly, when the matter is first reported to a family court, we are in a circumstance where the reporter, most often a mother, is not only disbelieved by a court, but she becomes the focus of the investigation. The mother tends to naively report what the child has disclosed to her and anticipates that her child will be believed and protected. Instead, she finds herself the focus of an attack. Rather than granting the child protection, the court does not accept the mother's reports of the child's words. Sometimes a forensic evaluator is assigned to evaluate all of the parties in the divorce action, rather than appoint a specially trained evaluator to assess only with regard to the issue of abuse.

At this very first step in family court, any future potential for a criminal investigation may be tainted such that it would make future prosecution impossible, in part because an evaluation of child abuse does not require evaluating the named perpetrator. See APSAC Practice Guidelines (American Professional Society on the Abuse of Children, 2012). But it is at this stage that a court should carefully protect the interests of a potential future prosecution.

When a custody evaluation is performed, rather than an abuse-specific evaluation, the focus is on the parents rather than on the allegations made by the child. In one typical scenario, the father denies abusing the child and accuses the mother of being overly angry at him; he alleges that the mother created a "story," coached the child, and is seeking to interfere with his wonderful relationship with the child.

Too frequently, the court orders the mother not to discuss the child's allegations with the child. The child, who trusted the mother enough to disclose, has his trusted parent essentially removed as a confidant.

In that scenario, the father likely continues seeing the child. It is possible the judge has ordered supervised visitation for the father. In that circumstance, there is a negative message to reporter of abuse and to the child. The mother who reported feels unsupported while the father, the named abuser, is likely to feel believed and empowered. The child, who loves the father despite the abuse, may feel safe with a supervisor present and may never disclose again. In this scenario, it is even more imperative that an expert understand the science of disclosure and the behavior of an abused child.

An abused child may have been threatened. An abused child may fear a parent going to jail and feel responsible. Science is critical.

Another scenario involves a named perpetrator being admonished by the court not to abuse and nothing is done to intervene with regular visitation. This "set up" by the court is ludicrous and unfortunately portends what follows. Anecdotally, sex abuse of a child by a parent in the middle of divorce may be the only crime where we ask a potential criminal if he committed the crime and rely upon his denial. This is too often what transpires in court. It may also be the only crime other than rape where we assume the victim is lying. Indeed, an abusive parent actually lives in a circumstance where his behavior can be repeated at will much like a career criminal who continues to "get away" with it. Would a court consider telling a career criminal to "knock it off" while an allegation is pending? But in child abuse cases, as in domestic abuse between spouses, courts tell abusers to stop abusing and actually rely upon their admonition not to abuse as if they really have that power. That admonition may be heard by the child molester as saying to the parent who reported the abuse as, "Liar liar! We don't believe you. This will be impossible to prove so you better give it up now."

Indeed, if anyone really believed a child was being molested, the molester would not be allowed to see the child. The assumption is that the father is right. The child's words are not at the forefront. The child's words get lost and are reported as if they were the mother's.

The father deflects and says things like, "I would never abuse" or "I would never do such a thing and mother has always had a problem with sex" (as if child rape and molestation is the equivalent of adult sex); or "I don't understand why the child (or mother) would say such a thing."

Frequently, when the perpetrator's words are examined carefully (and the web he has spun is unspun carefully), there is no actual denial of the abuse itself. In all of this, the father makes himself out to be a victim of mother's attacks as if she had a spurious motive. Even the evaluation of the child risks becoming focused on undoing the disclosures of the child; rather than learning about the abuse itself, the evaluator becomes preoccupied with trying to figure out why else the child might be accusing a father of abuse. This would not happen if experts were required to have science-specific knowledge or if this case was being criminally prosecuted.

The child loses his veracity as a first-hand reporter of something that happened to him. The child is not seen as a victim or treated as a victim; his words are parsed. This is reminiscent of when rape victims were permitted to be attacked on the witness stand with regard to their sex lives, as if sex and rape are synonymous. Because the child is not a party, this is difficult to attack. In addition because the bias of evaluators is so prevalent and so many child victims are placed with the named perpetrator, it is an exceedingly difficult paradigm to change.

With the child, the court should require someone with specialized training in interviewing children suspected of abuse. Again we emphasize: the science is critical. An expert can explain the scientific basis for why the child has reported in the way he has—how the experience of abuse appeared through the eyes of the child. Instead, the case in court becomes a "he said/she said," while the child's words are ignored. Thus, an evaluation in family court may make it virtually inevitable that there will not be a criminal prosecution even if abuse is found.

Why did this happen? In other areas of law, such as murder, we demand that science be used. Why in the area of family law is it permissible to ignore science? Perhaps the blame can be laid at the feet of ignorant lawyers and an unbalanced system of finances between parents, and the protective parent being essentially charged as if they were the "state"—the prosecution—to prove the case without the resources or knowledge of how to do so. Also to blame are untrained judges and their having dockets too large to give proper time.

Science has come to know that a child of approximately five to eight years old who reports abuse does not necessarily have a hidden agenda (Motzkau, 2007). In the vernacular, children "tell it like it is." We know perpetrators do not admit crimes against children. We know perpetrators often have multiple victims and they should never be alone with children. See the Association for the

Treatment of Sexual Abusers (2001) Professional Code of Ethics. We know it is the perpetrator of abuse of a child who threatens to harm the child or someone he loves and may mock the child, saying she won't be believed. We know children are confused by the abuse by a parent.

But once the report of abuse bypasses prosecution and goes to family court, the case gets twisted to focus on whether or not the mother gave a false report. The story told through the eyes of the child gets lost.

The country has read the very public and heartfelt story of the now adult Dylan Farrow (Kristof, 2014), who reported to her mother when she was a mere seven years old that she was being molested by her father. She is an adult now. And as an adult, she has openly and courageously used her own words to tell her story of childhood molestation. She expresses her pain and her fear as well as her own mother's support and love.

In some legal circles Dylan Farrow has been attacked because her mother elected not to seek prosecution. There, she is not heard in the voice she used to tell of her experiences and her pain. She is being attacked now as a liar as though as an adult she is still the victim of an angry mother. She is not treated as an adult woman telling something about her personal history. As with many of these cases, facts get twisted and misused.

In all child sexual abuse cases between parents that I have seen there is a dichotomy. The words and reality of the child become attacked and undermined as though they are the mother's allegations. Even now, so many years later, Dylan Farrow seems almost anonymous in telling her story, as though it is not her story at all. When science is replaced with emotion, children are not put first.

We call on all mental health professionals who care about children to demand science in their community, and when children report abuse to them or to a parent, that that they advocate for the child and promote prosecution and demand science from their colleagues who investigate allegations.

[12]

THE "BEST INTEREST" STANDARD VERSUS CHANGING THE STANDARD TO ASSURE CHILD SAFETY

Do we recognize that the issue of child abuse gets raised in only about 1–2% of all cases in family courts? Do we realize that disproportionally 65–70% of these children who make allegations of abuse during custody litigation get placed in the custodial care of the accused parent (Saunders, 2011)? Do we realize that, in most of these cases, there is a mental health professional who has made that recommendation of custody to the abuser, and that the court listened and followed that professional's recommendation?

How can it happen that mental health professionals make recommendations that children are placed with their abuser (Saunders, 2011)? These so-called experts have essentially become accomplices to the abuser, no different from the football and administrative communities at Penn State that protected Sandusky as more and more people were abused. In Sandusky's case, individual people in the broader Penn State community wielded tremendous power to disempower the children and to deflect attention from what they knew or should have known Sandusky was doing to his victims. So, too, experts, often improperly trained, wield that same power in our family courts even as children are sent to live with their abusers. This too comes from inadequate training as well as bias.

In family court, these so-called experts deflect blame from the abuser to the protective parent, even when we know most children do not lie and do not raise these issues falsely. The children are ignored. They get sent home to be abused, despite the fact that it is easy enough to distinguish between actually traumatized children and those with a false story about abuse. It is in the financial interest of the so-called experts who conduct these evaluations, absent specialized knowledge, to continue the status quo just as it was at Penn State to keep football alive as a thriving business.

Fundamental values must be examined to try to make change. Football is big business. That big business was more important than the welfare of any individual child. Only when the number of children being abused by the same man became too large to ignore was the problem properly examined. In family court, both the prevalent and implicit value is in keeping the status quo by using the outmoded standard of "best interest," even when a child has made an accusation of abuse.

"Best interests" is statutory language used as a guide to determine which parent is better suited as a primary or sole custodian of a child in cases in which parents cannot agree on the issue. It varies from state to state and considers various criteria. Some of these criteria are (1) the relative stability of each parent's home, (2) opportunities for the child's social life, (3) which parent is better able to provide appropriate care for the child, and (4) who the child looks to for love, attention, and support. Which one if either is the child's primary parent? Which is the child's psychological parent? A key element to most of these guides is also which parent can foster the love, affection, and support of the other parent. This last element easily becomes victim to abusers who too often can maintain their composure and appear loving and supportive of the other parent, while the parent who was actually victimized is regularly found to be too angry to foster a loving relationship with the other parent. Either the impact of the violence in the home on the child or the allegations by the child of abuse often get set aside and are never examined independently. The best interest standard purports to be for the child, but in essence it is a standard that creates a contest between competing parental rights and interests. The issue of the friendly parent to the other becomes "who appears best," and the appropriate anger of a parent who is victim of domestic abuse or of a child alleging abuse gets used against that parent in portraying him or her as unable to foster a loving relationship with the abusive parent. This standard should be irrelevant when there is domestic abuse and when a child has alleged abuse by a parent; however, the status quo maintains the integrity of the courts' standards for best interests to determine custodial relationships. Courts settle disputes between warring parents while the issues of child abuse take a back seat. We would hope that where child abuse rears its ugly head, this would be the highest priority that the family court would address, yet some experts participate in promulgating a cover-up and enhance their own financial well-being in doing so.

Indeed, addressing the issue of risk to child safety before applying the principle of best interest might resolve most of the emotional, as well as some of the legal, issues in a typical matrimonial case, thus eliminating the need for a trial. The issue must be safety of children first. Parental rights must come second to the protection of children. In no circumstances should experts benefit financially by placing the rights of paying parents ahead of the welfare of children. To do so means that neither the court nor psychologist is addressing the child's true best interests, as any reasonable person understands that someone who abuses a child cannot provide for the child's best interests.

There is social acceptance rather than outrage, much the same as the cover-up done by some in charge at Penn State who had knowledge and chose to ignore it. It is easy to ascribe blame and more difficult to take personal responsibility. It is easy to look the other way, more difficult to try to figure out how to change it. To understand the problem requires that we all take a fresh look at how the family courts operate and recognize that we have a role in the cover-up where we know and choose to do nothing.

Psychologists play a pivotal role in the decision to give custody of abused children to their perpetrators when they have made such a recommendation. It also becomes impossible to prosecute these crimes. In virtually every family court case where a child is placed in the custody of an abuser, there has been a so-called expert who has opined it is in that child's best interests. Once this is done, all competing allegations by the child are projected onto the protective parent and the allegations are ignored as a fabrication or a lie, or attributed to some unscientific phenomena. This may even be worse than the Sandusky cover-up because we are promulgating false premises to the court and teaching judges flawed science. These same judges then use this "knowledge" the next time an issue is raised and the cover-up continues.

Whose job is it to assure that the children are safe? The experts' job would be unnecessary as to best interests if there were no allowance of risk to the child after a child has made an allegation. Instead, the expert appointed by the court, aware of the legal standard of best interests that the judge must use, would conduct an evaluation of abuse and risk to safety. Specialized knowledge would then be required. It is against the financial interest of the status quo.

Psychologists can take leadership by reframing best interests as an impossible psychological standard whenever safety issues are raised by a child. Safety, without risk to the child, should be society's standard. Could we send "some" children to be with Sandusky, and still believe he would not hurt "our" child if indeed we knew he was hurting "some" children? Would any psychologist take that risk for his or her own child?

Psychologists can begin to set standards by using what is known in the literature about allegations of abuse, determining whether or not there is any risk, and then advocating for child safety, rather than balancing risks to determine a false premise of best interests. Where the question of abuse is raised by a child, best interests means balancing the risk of a child living with an appropriately angry and protective parent, versus living with a named abuser. It is the child, not the protective parent, making an accusation. By recommending that the child live even part-time with that abuser, a psychologist participates in the crime by increasing risk of harm to that very child.

There is no accountability for the expert making such a recommendation unless there is outrage and change. These very experts are given immunity, allowing them to continue to promulgate these false premises to the courts. We need to train psychologists in trauma, including the impact of a child's exposure to violence in the home and how to determine whether a child is a victim of abuse himself. In many cases, the trainers themselves are part of the problem, because so many of those who do the training espouse junk science, and then teach judges and other experts that junk science, rather than teaching what is known in the large body of literature about how to determine true allegations of abuse.

For one well documented example, the late Dr. Richard Gardner, a psychiatrist, is the founder and original formulator of what he called the "parent alienation syndrome." On cross-examination, and after ten years of "educating" the judges and mental health professionals, it was determined that his "syndrome" was not recognized in the mental health community

Despite being roundly rebuked by the mental health community, there are cases across the country where social workers, mental health professionals, and courts invoke this junk science to take children from protective parents and place them with abusers.

Anecdotally, in hundreds of cases the author Kleinman was involved in, this junk science was raised as a defense in virtually every case in which child abuse is raised against the father. Unfortunately, it gains traction and greatly skews the result when protective parents seek child protection.

We are not arguing here about "parent alienation syndrome" (PAS). This has been soundly debunked (Walker & Shapiro, 2010). Nonetheless, it is accepted by many judges throughout the country as a valid basis for punishing a protective parent (usually mother) and making custody and visitation decisions that regularly return an abused child to an "at risk" circumstance, now referring to it simply as parent alienation.

Trainers of judges and other young psychologists too often use this methodology as well to train evaluators. In doing so, they are not only using bad science, they are promulgating abuse. There is a dichotomy here: On the one hand, science has the knowledge and the know-how to ascertain coaching of child witnesses and the likelihood of abuse, even where there are no physical signs; on the other hand, the courts like psychologists to make things simple. It would be simple if child safety and no risk were the standard for best interests. It would be simple if all psychologists were properly trained and junk science was not permitted in the form of PAS and other made-up phenomena. Instead, to assist courts, and with no scientific basis to do so, some psychologists try to measure risk where none can be measured, using legal standards as opposed to scientific data.

It cannot be ignored that some psychologists reap the rewards of making it easier for the court. They are paid well and receive multiple appointments and their names get circulated among other judges. In this equation psychologists too often measure the risk of the parent who is protective and the impact of her anger at the abusive parent where no measurement is appropriate or warranted and there is no science to back it up. When the child is being harmed, the issue of risk to his or her safety takes a back seat to the anger of the protective parent. The voice of the child is lost. The protective parent's anger becomes the focus of the evaluation instead of applying what is known about false allegations, that is, the manner in which it is proper to determine whether allegations are true as told by the child, rather than measuring the parent's anger.

There is a body of literature on false allegations and on how to determine if children are telling the truth or being coached (Lyon & Dente, 2012; Lindsay, 2007), all of which gets set aside when untrained people do evaluations and use the false premise of best interests before looking at abuse.

[13]

THE INTERSECTION
OF FORENSIC OPINION AND
THERAPIST TESTIMONY

One of the most difficult tasks for any trial attorney during a contested child custody case is determining who should testify and in
what capacity. Once it is determined that an expert opinion will
be of assistance to the court, the lawyer must choose what type
of expert will be most beneficial: a forensic evaluator or a treating
therapist. However, questions often arise from reluctant treating
therapists when they are asked to testify. We query whether there
should be any dilemma.

For the court, an individual can be qualified to testify and give
opinion testimony as an expert so long as they have more than a
lay person's knowledge of the subject matter. All psychologists pre-
sumably meet that standard and thus the question for the attorney
is merely whether or not an evaluation of an individual or individuals will yield the desired information for the case before the
court. If not, would it be better to have someone's therapist testify
instead of, or in addition to, a forensic evaluator?

In domestic abuse and child protection cases, the answer as
to who testifies is a critical one and it may make the difference

between a child being protected by the court or the court placing a child "at risk" in the home of a batterer or a child abuser. Most frequently a therapist is a crucial conduit to the court understanding the totality of a victim's circumstance.

It is well known that many forensic evaluators are selected by courts to perform custody evaluations. Many of these people are not sufficiently trained in areas of trauma to be evaluating individuals who suffer from trauma and trauma-related illness, such as Battered Woman's Syndrome and child abuse.

Too often courts assume that the credential of licensure or equivalent degree is sufficient to make someone an expert. Too many lawyers don't know the distinctions, so they do not properly cross examine. The courts are then left to rely upon unqualified experts. In some states an attorney is not permitted to hire his or her own expert until a court appointed person renders an opinion. The litigant's expert then has an even more difficult task.

If the "underqualified" forensic evaluator renders an unsupported opinion because he lacks requisite knowledge or expertise to have conducted an evaluation of a domestic abuse or child abuse issue in the first place, a therapist for the battered spouse or abused child can counter this inadequacy. The therapist can create context, give documented history, and also correct inaccurate interpretations. Doing so may change the perception of the court without it appearing as if there is a war of the experts. Where the court has an expert first, the court will almost instinctively rely more heavily on someone it trusts or knows even when that individual lacks appropriate credentials. So having a therapist testify can also give an important perception that the battered spouse is not seeking to hide behind the shield of confidentiality even in a situation in which it can be done appropriately.

How often do treating therapists of child victims who asked to testify feel they are qualified to testify as an expert because they may not know the entirety of a case or have a balanced position, or they are confused about the ethical requirement of confidentiality if they render an opinion? To testify does require consent of the client, and balance is not necessary. They must seek and get permission of the client before testifying to otherwise confidential information. But they can then explain why a child, for example, may not have told details of abuse, yet told the therapist during the course of treatment. Or they may be able to explain why a battered spouse never called the police or told a family member about what they were enduring. The therapist ought to be eager to assist in setting forth the issues as they are seen through their eyes only. In doing so they are not only supporting the patient but also giving validity in an open and concrete way.

By definition treating therapists are qualified to testify. They don't need to know the whole case. They have an obligation to improve the mental health of their patient and do what is in the patients' best interest. The treating therapist can only be examined by lawyers or the court with regard to issues about which they have sufficient information and expertise. They cannot be challenged as a forensic expert as they are not required to be balanced. They are treating, not evaluating.

What a therapist is treating for, and how they determined what treatment is necessary as a result of what they observe clinically, is important on many levels. First, from an evidentiary standpoint, information gathered during therapy, which is told to a therapist in confidence during treatment by a child or an adult, is assumed to be honest and for the sole purpose of treatment. Thus, this information, when testified to in court by a treating therapist, may be less suspect than the identical information given to an evaluator by the same person, be it a child or an adult.

Second, the opinion of a child's therapist with regard to what happened to a child, when child abuse is alleged for example, and when a child has revealed abuse to the therapist, may be the most powerful and persuasive testimony for a court to hear. It is known that children often do not re-disclose the same information twice. Especially young children may believe one adult has communicated the information to the other and they don't tell again. Abuse does not get told by children as a "story." The information comes out over a period of time and leaves many unanswered questions. This may be disconcerting or not believed by the untrained psychologist. Therapists become trusted adults in a child's life, and thus may be given more detailed information than a forensic evaluator to whom the child may never disclose the same information in the same amount of detail.

In contrast to the therapist, the forensic evaluator may not have built sufficient rapport. An improperly trained forensic evaluator may not recognize the need for more rapport building. They may see disclosures by a child to someone else as lies or the result of coaching when the child has not specifically disclosed this information to them. The therapist, however, is likely to know the child better. In doing what is in the best interest of the client, the therapist is best positioned to speak about the child's disclosures and the likelihood of their being what the child actually experienced, and to give opinions to the court as to the child's level of suffering; or similarly, to speak of a battered wife's descriptions of her experience and why it fits with having been actually battered.

An evaluator may not have been directly told about the abuse by the child. The evaluator may thus have only heard about the disclosures of a child from a second-hand source, about whom the evaluator may be skeptical. If the mother is the second-hand source and is also a victim of spouse abuse, forensic evaluators with little or no training may inaccurately attribute expressions of anger or fear to vindictiveness and paranoia rather than recognizing them as symptoms of posttraumatic stress. A therapist may opine on these issues directly about their patient, thus negating a poorly done court-appointed evaluation's inaccurate findings.

While on the surface the problem for the therapist is revealing confidential information, that is not different from a forensic evaluator who must tell the person being evaluated that there is no information that can be kept confidential from the court once it is disclosed. Also, especially with domestic abuse and child abuse, the most difficult information to disclose may be the most pertinent to disclose in order to gain protection from the court.

Some say that the tools of the forensic evaluator safeguard an evaluation process and may even overcome insufficient credentials of an evaluator. We disagree. These tools include the use of collateral information from a variety of sources other than the individuals being evaluated, as well as psychological testing. Evaluators without the requisite knowledge and training cannot weigh the importance of the information they are given, nor can they necessarily use proper collateral information or testing, nor are they qualified to interpret the results. Indeed, experience is often used as a counter to training and education. But if they have been doing it wrong for years, no matter how many evaluations have been done, it does not overcome the lack of education and proper training. This means simply that they will continue to do it wrong and risk putting children in harm's way. Thus, unless opposing counsel knows that the code of ethics for psychologists requires the evaluator to have specialized knowledge and training in these areas, the court may never know the evaluator is not qualified. A treating therapist testimony can assist the court in sorting this out.

There are many issues confronting experts in court. But it is critical that therapists be willing to testify as experts to assist their clients, enhance the courts' understanding of the nature of abuse, and help protect children in the courts. There is no dilemma. Their opinions are relevant and may be essential.

[14]

CUSTODY EVALUATIONS, THERAPY, CHILD PROTECTION, AND ETHICS

It is important to consider the relationship between the mental health professional's ethics and the lawyer's strategy. Not infrequently they collide when dealing with children in the courts. One tends to think of an expert as someone hired by a lawyer or appointed by a court to render an opinion and give testimony to the court. We would rather think of such experts as required to be child advocates, hired to evaluate parties and children, and then to serve the welfare of children, especially where the child needs special protection.

Child custody cases are unique, especially when the mental health professional concludes that the safety of a minor may be at risk. State law and professional ethics may require disclosure of confidential information that would ordinarily remain within the control of the lawyer.

The vast majority of child custody cases in family court are amicably resolved between the parents. However, within the small percentage of cases that become highly litigated, issues of violence are frequently raised. Therefore, these are the cases where a mental health professional's opinion and specialized knowledge are required.

Questions arise when abuse of a child becomes a concern of the mental health professional. While such professionals may be a part of a legal team, to be used by the lawyer in putting on his case, a mental health professional also has independent ethical obligations. For example, a psychologist is a mandated reporter of abuse. Therefore, whether the psychologist is hired by a party or ordered by a court to conduct an evaluation, the obligation to report abuse or risk thereof to a state agency remains the same. This is true even if the abusive parent hired the psychologist. The APA Practice Guidelines make clear that for psychologists, the child's welfare is paramount when conducting child custody evaluations.

All reporters of child abuse may remain anonymous. Some questions are raised:

1. After making a report, do mental health professionals have a continuing obligation of any sort to that child, to the law, or to their own ethical responsibility?

2. Do mental health professionals who make a mandated report of abuse during or after an evaluation have any additional obligation to the child, especially when there is ongoing legal action for custody between parents?

3. If so, what type of action is both ethical and permissible at law?

4. Are there ethical or legal parameters for taking action or for inaction?

5. Is a line drawn independently to define what is required or permitted by ethics versus the law?

These are essential questions to ask because there is an innate or tacit belief that courts get it right, that judges are trained to understand children and act in their best interests. When these same courts are weighing fairness between parents, how can judges simultaneously protect the safety of a child? It is as if they are being asked to prosecute and defend the same person. The child's safety may actually end up taking a back seat.

What then can mental health professional do? Where a professional is hired by the court, it may be easier to communicate concerns about one parent being a risk to the welfare of a child directly to the court. But where the professional is hired by one of the parties to the custody dispute, to communicate independently to the court would be impermissible, both ethically and legally. Action would be and should be initiated by the lawyer representing the party. But does that action, even if taken by a lawyer, fulfill the professional's ethical obligations as a psychologist? We think there must be a separate obligation.

For example, what happens when a lawyer represents the abusive parent? As an ethical professional, how can that person behave ethically even when hired by an abusive parent? Is that professional violating any obligations if they take legal action to protect a child, even though the attorney has no obligation to bring his client's abusive actions to the court's attention? The professional must make a mandated and anonymous report. What can the professional do if the Child Protective Service Agency takes no action or if that action/inaction screener is inept for some reason? The dilemma is there. The answer is more difficult.

To provide a link between ethics and the law we believe that the professionals should sign a contract before commencing an evaluation. Mental health professionals must maintain ethical standards during the evaluation even without this contract, but signing a contract would make the ethics and standards clear, especially where it turns out that the person who hired the psychologist has been abusing a child.

The contract could be between the professional and the parties hiring the evaluator. The contract could detail the professional's ethical duty to place the child's best interests above either of the parties. It could also specify that confidentiality may be breached in order to report to CPS if it is believed, based on evidence discovered in the process of evaluating the child, that there has been abuse or a risk of abuse. The professional should then also advise each party of the duty to report abuse in the general information given at the first evaluative session. The contract could also specify other conditions the professional requires. The contract would then be a memorandum of understanding between the parties regarding the professional's ethical duties and legal mandate to report, without which the evaluator would not engage in this work.

This is also true when a professional is appointed by the court to provide therapy for a child. The ethics of the professional must be adhered to, even at risk of losing the appointment by the court. Courts often do not know the ethical guidelines for different mental health professionals and do not understand the distinctions between these and law. The professionals have a duty to clarify this for the court and only to abide by their code of ethics— indeed to remove themselves from a case rather than to violate their ethics.

The contract should permit the professionals to go beyond what is required by ethical guidelines if, in their opinion, it is required to seek to secure a child's welfare. Doing so would follow the ethical requirement to keep a child's welfare at a higher priority than the needs of the other parties, but also would permit him to take whatever action he thinks is appropriate based upon the information he gathers during the evaluation. If there is such a contract, there would be no negative repercussions, even if the professional was were hired by the abusive parent.

The contract, if signed, alleviates other dilemmas. For example, where the appointment for an evaluation comes from a court and the court has taken no protective action, there may be other legally permissible actions available to the mental health professional. In some jurisdictions a professional may ask a prosecutor to conduct an independent investigation.

Some states permit anyone with an interest in a child to initiate a child protection matter. In New Jersey, for example, a psychologist could become an "interested party" and as such actually request the child protection agency to file a child protection case, separate from a custody matter, even if the agency has not seen it sufficient to file one on its own, after a report of abuse. Indeed, the language of the statute in New Jersey would be likely to permit the psychologist to become a plaintiff in such a matter. There may be other states with mechanisms for similar action. Such action could not now be taken in most circumstances because of the limited parameters placed on the psychologist when entering a case. This may also be cost-prohibitive for the plaintiff psychologist if a state agency does not prosecute the claims.

Additional ethical issues are raised where the abuse has been reported and investigated by the agency and even tried by a court to conclusion and a court has found there was no abuse. In most civil or criminal cases, where a matter has been concluded through trial, the law presumes the factual issue(s) are resolved for all times. This is referred to as *res judicata*. *Res judicata* would ordinarily settle the defining issues between parties. Moreover, in these civil cases, not involving child safety, the court has no special continuing obligations to the litigants.

But in a child custody or child protection matter, there is an open issue as long as there are minor children. When determining child safety, the court sits in a *parens patriae* role as the child's ultimate parent/protector. Accordingly, child abuse presents a distinct and separate risk, in that a "finding" may not resolve the issues of child safety for all time. The abuse itself may continue or injuries from past abuse may be recurring despite a case being resolved in the court.

The mental health professional needs to be following his own ethical guidelines, which may not neatly coincide with what a court has already understood. When a mental health professional evaluates a child or parent and finds abuse, despite what a court has found, he must be an advocate rather than a neutral observer. The first obligation is to present findings to the court. If the professional has clearly specified his ethical duty to place the child's welfare above the interests of any other parties, the attorneys and their clients will know in advance not to expect otherwise. The difficulty arises when the opposing attorney or the court takes action to disallow the finding of abuse.

We have seen mental health professionals elect to take proactive roles and lawyers look askance at this. But, if the professional believes a child is at risk even after a mandated report, it is important for the professional to understand that a state child protection agency is essentially a screening device. Where the investigator at the agency does not feel that a particular report rises to the level of abuse, the investigation may end with a screening for no further investigation. Some states permit the initial screening to rule out any investigation beyond the report. If there was a prior investigation of abuse, the new investigation may get short shrift, and in some states, they actually may turn their eyes to the other parent, about whom no concerns of abuse have ever been raised.

What then may a mental health professional do? First and foremost, the professional should submit her findings of past abuse or risk of abuse to the court. Each state is unique and it is the obligation of the professional who works within the framework of forensics to know what legal action may be available to him. The problem is that many attorneys and courts put fairness to the parties ahead of the welfare of the child, and some mental health professional behave unethically in performing child custody evaluations.

Noteworthy, in all circumstances, is the risk to a career, when one steps outside the bounds of what typically goes on in the courts, even if the behavior and action is both legal and ethical. If the mental health professional takes independent action she may never get appointed by a court again or asked by a lawyer to do another evaluation in the future. If her practice depends primarily on family court evaluations, her livelihood may be in jeopardy. On the other hand, if she does not take action, a child may continue to be injured or fail to get the protection he needs.

Mental health professionals need to think carefully about the collision of ethics between unscrupulous attorneys who hire them and their obligation to protect a child. The ethical responsibility to give the child's welfare highest priority can be clarified in writing and agreed to by all parties in advance of undertaking an assignment for an evaluation.

Once an evaluation is done and child abuse or risk of abuse is determined, a professional has statutory rules and ethical guidelines that require proactive behavior. What are some options? They can alert a pediatrician or call a prosecutor. In a worst case scenario of the psychologist hired by an abusive parent, the psychologist at minimum makes a mandated report. Thereafter, the mental health professional may elect not to write a written report for the lawyer. If subpoenaed by the other attorney the professional would have a duty, however, to acknowledge opinions regarding abuse and not attempt to protect her financial interest or the abusive parent.

Where the mental health professional is hired by a protective parent and has made a mandated report, the professional then has additional obligations to pursue safety for the child, the basis of which is the same basis upon which mandated reports have been required by the state law in every state. That is, it is anticipated that based upon training and experience and the special circumstances, he will during the course of his evaluation be able to elicit and interpret information in ways that would otherwise be confidential and may never otherwise be reported. His unique circumstance is that he may gather together much information from his own contacts, collaterals, possibly mandated interviews with the parents and other sources and prior medical records as well as traditionally confidential communications. When a child's welfare is at stake, it is not ethical simply to be an arm of a legal team. Whether hired by good lawyers or bad, the psychologist's obligation is to do a competent and ethical evaluation. If the professional determines the hiring attorney is unethical, she can remove herself from the case and not remain beholden to either the lawyer or to the individual who paid for the services.

All mental health professionals engaged in forensic work have an independent obligation to familiarize themselves with the laws of the state and adhere to the ethical guidelines for protecting a child's welfare. But there is a difference between ethics and guidelines. While guidelines are professionally used to guide, they may also be encompassed within state law, and some guidelines may be essential to follow. For example, American Professional Society on the Abuse of Children (APSAC) is an organization that publishes the accepted protocols for evaluation and treatment of children who have been abused. It also sets guidelines for the evaluation and treatment for children who may have been abused. It seeks to determine the validity, one way or the other, of the child's statements. Ultimately, the issue of child abuse comes from the child and through the eyes of the child—not the protective parent.

[15]

MENTAL HEALTH PROFESSIONALS TAKE RISKS WHEN EVALUATING CHILDREN

Many competent and ethical mental health professionals who have worked in the field of child protection and child evaluative forensics have come under personal and professional attack. These attacks come from attorneys of accused parents, organized groups, and sometimes licensing boards. The organized groups are often referred to as fathers' rights groups. However, the issue here is not about good fathers sharing parental rights.

Rather, these self-identified fathers' rights groups may seek to vindicate abusers by attacking good mothers and the professionals who work to protect children who have disclosed abuse. These attacks are mounted under the guise of giving equal rights to fathers. Too often these organizations and their members find ways to intimidate licensing boards, which then succumb to the pressure and file complaints against good mental health professionals. The professionals then become victims of multiple complaints because of their good work. This is targeting. Targeted mental health professionals spend an inordinate amount of time and money to maintain their practices and their dignity. As a

result of targeting, we have watched fewer mental health professional willing to step forward to evaluate and protect children who
have disclosed sexual, physical, and emotional abuse, especially
during divorce. All mental health professionals should be aware of
this pitfall. Yet it is imperative that these specially trained professionals continue to evaluate children. Avoiding evaluating these
children can be an asset to hate groups. Silence becomes a form of
advocacy for abusers. Only with proper evaluations can we prosecute perpetrators for injuring children. Only with properly conducted evaluations can children be protected. And only when we
meet this issue head-on can we stop these false complaints.

There is an apparent schism between the world of mental health
and the framework of the court, but it can be reconciled. A court
cannot interfere with someone's right to parent without a showing
that the child is at risk in his care. But the manner in which a custody evaluation is conducted is in the purview of the evaluator and
should be done pursuant to professional guidelines and scientific
understanding. It is a child's disclosure which generally raises the
issue of abuse, and that disclosure is brought to court by a parent.
The courts, however, in the interest of "fairness" to both parents
seem to believe that fairness requires that a named perpetrator
be interviewed in the presence of the child even where the professional guidelines to assess abuse do not require it. Too frequently
the courts appoint people to conduct evaluations in accord with
a court's notion of fairness. Thereafter, the courts make negative
judgments and inferences about the abuse as a result of improperly
done evaluations with reliance placed on untested or false criteria.
This happens especially where a child does not repeat the allegations or if they appear comfortable with a named perpetrator.

It is up to an evaluator to make the court aware that, for example, APSAC says that the primary information of sexual abuse

comes from the child him/herself; that the named abuser should not be present or bring a child to an interview; and it is not necessary to interview the accused parent. APSAC guidelines do not require that a person accused of child sexual abuse even be interviewed to determine whether or not a child has been abused by that parent. The APSAC literature explains, for example, that a child appearing comfortable in the presence of a sexually abusive parent is not an indicator that the abuse did not occur. But the fact that a child appears comfortable with a named perpetrator gets used in courts every day to accuse mothers of coaching that child, and/or lying even where no evidence of coaching exists. It is used to deny abuse. The mental health professional doing an investigative interview must intervene, explain, and teach the court. Only then can psychology and the law be reconciled to protect children.

A mental health professional should not succumb to court notions of fairness where the professional standards demand otherwise. Instead the professional can teach the court proper standards of practice. During a custody evaluation it is appropriate to interview both parents with and without the child. However, take the circumstance where a custody evaluation is performed and a child may have appeared comfortable with a parent. That same parent is later accused of sexual abuse by that same child. It is up to the expert who opines that there is abuse of that child by that parent to explain to the court in a report that no inference of abuse can be made from the fact that the child appeared comfortable with the perpetrator.

It may be difficult to understand why, for example, the children who Sandusky is alleged to have abused repeatedly continued to go with him cheerfully. It is up to the psychologist to explain this phenomenon. Custody statutes vary state to state. Some states, often referred to as "friendly states," contain a presumption that in divorce, parents should co-parent as joint custodians. Other states have presumptions, for example, that where there is domestic abuse, custody should be with the non-violent parent. It is well accepted in all states that there is a correlation between spousal abuse and child abuse, yet invariably courts express surprise when child abuse is raised during divorce, even where spouse abuse is found to have occurred, even at times where restraining orders have been granted.

The evaluation report of abuse should contain an answer to presumed skepticism with which a child abuse report will be met. By doing this, one can begin to combat the inordinate amount of disbelief that may come when child abuse is raised, especially in a divorce. In divorce court, absent a mental health report that opines the child was abused, these matters become "he said/she said" cases and too often the children's voice is lost in the process. Prosecution then becomes impossible. But a properly conducted evaluation of a child, upon a child's initial disclosure, can take a child's words and contextualize them for a court. The opinion of an expert matters.

How many of our parents were told as a child; "stand up to the bully on the playground; act like you are not afraid; the bully is more afraid than you are or they would not bully; face them and they will back down." Each of us learned an important life lesson. Competent mental health professionals can become aware of the pitfalls of doing these critical evaluations and must be willing to face down the bully when necessary by continuing to practice in this field. If professionals who are attacked openly share their experiences of attack with each other and come to one another's professional aid, then the bullies can be faced down and children can be protected.

There is no way to stop the attacks against protective parents and child advocates. There is a way to defend against them—to be familiar with the professional literature, to be prepared with proper reports to the courts in advance of attack, to be faithful to professional standards, and to come to each other's aid when attacked.

[16]

DOMESTIC ABUSE AND CHILD PROTECTION

Is What We Are Doing Working?

We ask ourselves, "Is what we are doing working? And who are *we*?" Perhaps identifying specific issues will help:

- How should we measure success?
- How do we know if what we are doing is working?
- Are more children safe?
- Are more battered women able to protect their children?
- Are the courts more sensitive now than they were ten years ago? five years ago?
- Are more lawyers familiarizing themselves with the impact of domestic abuse on children?
- Are more psychologists/evaluators better able to assess the impact of violence on children and render opinions to courts that give the courts the information they need to protect children?

Indeed, the measurement of success is complex. In a court-room, these issues regularly fall back to the issue of parental rights versus safety of a child in a contested matrimonial forum. Since an abuser is often more financially capable of driving and surviving the litigation, what can a protective parent do to seek child protection? Protective parents need to find the power they have and then learn to use it effectively. The community that thinks about this issue and attempts to help *is* the power that protective parents have and the power they are using. They are meeting and sharing experiences. There are listservs and blogs. We are researching, listening, reading, and learning, and we, who care, are growing in numbers.

We are still facing the difficult challenges of litigation, the bias of the community, amid the refusal of many to integrate what is known about stranger violence with family violence. The old and romanticized notions of fathers who injure their families but claim to want to spend more time with their children is becoming understood as a misuse of power. While many laws on the books are still not properly implemented and junk science concepts still exist in many jurisdictions, we are seeing changes being made.

We often see a point where the court seems to change focus from child protection to the parental rights of the litigants. As the matter proceeds, it appears the protective parent then becomes labeled as the "uncooperative parent." But protective parents are stronger today than yesterday. Many changes in the courts have taken place. Many still face the challenges of losing children to abusers, and many are still embattled in unfair family courts. Even judges are acknowledging errors and missteps.

Change has come slowly. Many feel impaled by the courts. Those parents labeled uncooperative, unreasonable, too angry to settle, or too hostile to have joint custody have risked losing in efforts to protect their children. Since 70% of the protective parents risk losing not only custody, but also visitation and contact with their children, the point that changes the focus from child protection to parental rights has to be moved toward child protection (Saunders et al., 2011).

In spite of many frustrations and personal horror stories, the landscape across the country is changing. In 1980, there was no 911. Today, police respond to a 911 domestic abuse call immediately and take security action between the parties in a manner that was impossible and unheard of 30 years ago.

Domestic abuse laws do protect many women and children.

We must keep the issues of intimate violence and child abuse alive and in the public eye. As we keep talking about bias in the courts and the tragedies of tearing children from loving parents as a means of controlling supposedly uncooperative parents, we become part of the landslide of informants on a national scale.

With pressure, intimate-violence training in public and private spheres will move forward ever more quickly. Courts and legislators will listen if a public outcry is consistent, since these issues affect everyone in their district.

This is not a woman's movement. It is a movement to ensure the safety and protection of children. There are icons in this movement, but every person, doing their part by doing a proper court evaluation, is educating the court and the public about the schism between the law and its implementation. We have grown and we have changed. What is being done is working. In writing and speaking and confronting these issues, we restore my own faith in community and a system that must succeed for all of us, but especially our children.

[17]

CONCLUSION

An Open Letter to a Young Lawyer: A Critical
Look at the Child Custody System
and What Every Mental Health Person
Should Know about Lawyers

Dear Jenn,

You are about to graduate from law school. Congratulations!
Graduation is are both a beginning and an end. Your experience has
taught you to read differently, write persuasively, think resolutely,
and to know there are more than two sides to every story. It has
taught you that the law is whatever the court says it is unless someone appeals and the appellate authority changes it. Then it remains
the law unless and until a higher authority changes it again or the
legislature says differently. Then it remains that way unless the
Supreme Court determines something was determined incorrectly,
misunderstood, or wrong. The law is an evolving, changing concept,
subject to social pressure and scientific nuances, modification, clari-
fication, influence—always with a sense of purpose and hope.

You now feel wise and you should. You can tackle problems
with aplomb; you can research and come to understand and

advocate positions. You feel supported and secure. You have spent three years studying diligently and are about to enter a new world, a world where you can confront change, make law, and affect society.

So, as I sit down to write to you, for your special day, I want to give you a special gift, a gift that I have given to no one, a gift you can carry with you as you work hard and think problems through, and work to make our world a better place and then decide to share it as well. It is not a feel-good gift, but one that comes from the heart.

Jenn, you care about people. You care about justice. You care that society brings justice to all. So why have I titled this letter in a way that brings images of fantasy rather than reality? I have done so because I want to tell you about the other face of the law, the face that as a lawyer you will see daily.

I learned that working for change, one case at a time, is insufficient. A broader approach is needed, one that sensitizes judges and court personnel to the uniqueness of each case and the harm that can result for children from uninformed rulings. You will learn that family court fails children and society at large, especially when a woman protective of her children is involved and more so where there has been domestic abuse.

Why?

There are many concerns surrounding the issue of child custody determinations worthy of special attention. Among them are the system's lack of time to attend to critical issues due to the number of cases each judge must attend to; the lack of necessary resources, or sometimes even the ability to assess what resources are necessary; and the requirement that a judge essentially become an expert deciding on the welfare of children and their future, deciding where and how they will live. The judicial process is a bit like the Wizard of Oz's smoke, ropes, and whistles. It is almost as though unless there is the right court, judge, lawyers, experts—all in the right state and at the right time—one should stay away from family court.

Judges are mortals. They are placed in the role of determining lives of children when parents are unable to resolve issues for themselves. As soon as one parent raises the issue of custody or visitation before a court, both parents lose their right to direct, select, and determine the lives of their own children.

We place an awesome burden upon that judge to somehow sufficiently understand our lives and the lives of our children and determine who is right, who is wrong, and what is best. We believe that justice will prevail, yet justice for our children requires someone we have never met to understand the nuances of our lives and, when child custody determinations are involved, to assess, treat, and decide with the wisdom of Solomon.

No one can believe that anyone could ever judge these cases to our satisfaction.

Our fortitude and belief in the system cannot withstand huge error or continuing error. We revere the judge as Dorothy did the Wizard. But judges are people. Cases begin with the creation of adversaries. The husband or wife filing a request to dissolve a marriage or resolve a custody issue becomes a plaintiff; the other party becomes a defendant. Virtually all family matters are resolved without a trial. Rare is the case where parents cannot ultimately figure out how to resolve family differences and create a circumstance in the best interest of their children. But it is this small percentage of cases about which we should feel the most concern. It may be a small percentage, but a large number nevertheless, and so many children whose lives are touched.

The system requires a judge, once a lawyer, to take classes with other judges on family law. Unfortunately, addressing these issues in class does not deal with the fatigue of these cases and their counter-intuitive nature. Some of these are men and women who may never have practiced family law or ever taken a class in psychology or social work. Still, they make interim decisions regarding where and with whom children should live. Sometimes they do so without testimony of the parents, based only on written and opposing certifications, declarations, or affidavits, with or without arguments of counsel and with no regard for the quality or experience of the attorneys or mental health professionals. In sum, a person who does not know the family and who does not necessarily meet the parents can make uninformed decisions based on the law and a few pages of writing by a stranger.

Since most people do not have dealings with lawyers, most of us do not know how to interview, much less select, someone competent. Then there are the financial constraints. But judges care about making the best decisions for each family.

When I was a law clerk years ago, the county where I worked estimated that 2,000 cases touched a family court judge's desk in a year. How can they care so much or for so many? Although most cases eventually settle somewhat amicably and without a trial, what happens beforehand will impact many young lives, as well as parents who find themselves unwittingly at the mercy of decisions made for them, decisions that they would have made differently if still in charge of their children.

I believe that as a lawyer, I can change things. I can help parents whose children are jeopardized by a violent or abusive parent. I learned that protective parents are often seen as aggressive. These parents naively believe that the system will straighten out the life that they endured; that a judge will understand what they, the protective parent, did not understand while living in the marriage. They believe that the a judge will fix the circumstance that the protective parent could not fix.

Within the family court system, there are many fine resources upon which judges can rely to assist them in making decisions, including men and women with more expertise than the judge. Some are specially trained to mediate, arbitrate, assess, and present solutions. Often they come from teams of probation officers, child welfare workers, or children and youth workers. Parents believe these people will know and understand and help them to protect. These parents reach out and tell their stories to them. The parents ask for help and tell of threats to them and to their children. Often the protective parent feels that the stories fall on deaf ears. And that is because these specially trained people do not have the time to deal with the complexity of issues that parents cannot ultimately resolve themselves. They are not "traumatologists" or experts in abuse dynamics or the impact on children of "staying one more day" with a perpetrator. These specialists, too, are mortals, in a system where most cases settle. This is the system. This is family court justice.

What then of a case that will not settle?

As the attorney, you may know the adversary parent cannot take "Yes" for an answer. Every time your client meets their demands, the other party ups the ante; they change the demand, they want more, and your client eventually says "No." She has lived with violence. Her children have lived it. But the children are aligning with their father against her. This woman's whole life has been geared to raising these children. Now they are 6, 8, 10, and 13, and she fears that she is about to lose them.

She gave up her career but was forced by circumstances to take a mere job. She made beds and stayed up at night and helped her husband through *his* career. For everyone, she balanced the calendar and the checkbook, trying to figure out where to borrow to pay the next mortgage payment, since she bought camp clothes for the children.

There were sleepless nights and late-night dinners for her husband after she fed the kids and did their homework, took them to practice, gave them baths, and put them to sleep. She endured no sleep when the kids were sick. After all, her husband had to sleep so he could climb the career ladder. She sewed buttons, and sweated through soccer and ballet. She stayed up late at night and begged her husband to come to a game. He seldom did. She urged the children to tell him how much they cared about his spending time with him. And they did care. And he now uses that against her. She begged her husband to spend moments of quality time with their children and he seldom did.

He berated her in front of the children and, for their sake, she took it. He hit her and she stayed. And now, when her husband hit their son, she could not take it anymore. So she left, believing the system would now help her. Instead, her husband now wants custody of the children and claims she is unfit. He says she is lying about the violence or at least about its impact. He accuses her of fighting and screaming a lot, which he claims made things worse. He says the kids want to be with him. He demands a custody hearing. She is scared and she is proud and she believes that justice will prevail and the judge will understand and maintain the status quo, with her as the parent in charge of their lives and her husband working and supporting the family and participating marginally in their lives as he has always done.

She goes to court and a judge sends the children to her husband for half the time. Ironically, she could never even get him to one of the kids' games. Now he gets to make decisions he would never even remotely discuss with her for the past 13 years.

Johnny is now in great distress, but she is not permitted to even choose a therapist for Johnny because her husband objects. She is hysterical and upset, and he is calm and demure. The judge sees her and worries about the kids; the judge sees him and knows he will be a good influence. The kids under her care were getting straight A's, and were thriving in after-school activities. She is about to lose her children and her world. But the judge knows best and gives him half time and looks at her askance because she seems hysterical and the judge thinks her husband is right, that she must be crazy.

She is hysterical because she has been abused and battered but the courts do not believe her; he has berated her, hit her, and called her names, all in front of the children, and it has hurt the kids. These experts, the judge and the court personnel who are supposed to know better, have failed.

Jenn, it is this woman and her family I worry about. And it is that case that you, too, will worry about. It is that part of the system that fails children.

When children are failed, society is failed. Where a judge misreads the signals, assumes he knows the family dynamics, but is wrong or there is no expert who understands and can explain it, and as a result a child goes unprotected, it is not enough to say it is alright.

We should revere the judge even as we recognize the frailties of the system. The judge is merely a man or woman doing a job with little training. We respond to the awesome power of the judge's role.

The magic is dealing with each case as though it is unique, each child as important, and treating each client with respect and concern. It means finding experts who know and who can be trusted to assist and to educate the court..

Part of the lawyer's awesome responsibility is to counsel wisely. Sometimes that means advising a client to stay away from the system and not take the risk of the judge getting it wrong.

Jenn, I reflect back so often on your time working with me: on our daily trips to New York, leaving early and coming home late after a continuing trial. We talked a blue streak, so often about whether or not you should consider law as a professional option.

We discussed the whys and wherefores and the fact that the law was as wide as your imagination. We discussed the difficulty of evidence issues, and hearsay problems, and sometimes what appeared to be different treatment toward the attorneys by the judge. I explained potential appellate issues as they were raised and the importance of strong advocacy. I reminded you of my credo, taught by my law school professor: If you are not pushing contempt, you are not properly advocating. On all those long conversations about the case and about the law, there is much I did not say then. I hope this letter helps fill some gaps.

I continue to believe that every child has the right to grow up in a safe environment, and I ask you to work to try to correct these flaws, to try to find the magic to shift these scenes, clear the smoke, and transform the language, so that we can see clearly and with one voice and one language we all can speak and trust. Then the judge can see clearly too and give all kids a real chance at having their best interests served by the family court.

Go get 'em Jenn.

[18]

KIDS GROW UP

Sixteen years ago, I left. Eight years ago was the end of litigation. Eight years ago, I remarried. One year ago, Sidney died. Today I walk in stores and see mothers with young children and wonder how I managed day-to-day with three children, no money, and fighting a legal battle. During the litigation, I managed to finish college.

Ramona is a junior in high school. Her relationship with her father never improved. He never apologized or recognized he had hurt her. As she got older, they went to dinner periodically on a birthday or other special day when her brothers were present. I think she felt sadness at his death, at the loss of possibility.

David seemed to make peace with his relationship with his father. He grew up too fast. Once he wrote a certification to the court on behalf of his sister, explaining to the judge that Ramona was really afraid to be alone with him and that I had not created that fear, as Sidney had said I had done. Peculiarly, during my litigation, my parents were the brunt of his attack. They were accused of manipulating me and controlling me.

Throughout eight years of litigation, I was not given credit for the court fight. He insisted it was my parents' battle and not mine. The truth is, I could not have done it without their support. But it was my fight and my redemption from his bondage. The fight gave me the strength to do what I had not done in my marriage—to stand up for myself. Had I done that, early on, I never would have married him, or perhaps, he never would have married me. In either case, having had three children, I have no regrets.

Randy is in college studying acting. I think he would agree that I gave him the tools to deal with a formidable father, while allowing him freedom to establish the best relationship he could. I think it will take years to come to peace with it all.

David is grown. We are close. He may never know how important he was to me during the litigation years. He was always honest. He probably suffered more than he let me know. But he is a great human being. I hope he feels peace.

Sidney took me to court two days before I remarried. It was his last stand. The children love my new husband and he never tried to interfere in their father's relationship.

They trust their own perceptions and have great relationships with each other and with me. If that is how one measures success, then I guess I won, after all. It has been a lifetime. I can finally breathe free.

REFERENCES AND SUGGESTED READING

Ammar, N., Orloff, L., Dutton, M., & Aguilar-Hass, G. (2005). Calls to police and police response: A case study of Latina immigrant women in the USA. *International Journal of Police Science and Management, 7*(4), 230–244.

APSAC. (2012). APSAC Practice Guidelines (American Professional Society on the Abuse of Children):Columbus, OH.

Baker, L., & Jaffe, P. (2006). *A teacher's handbook: Understanding woman abuse and its effects on children. Strategies for responding to students.* London, Canada: Centre for Children & Families in the Justice System.

Bancroft, L. (2004). *When dad hurts mom: Helping your children heal the wounds of witnessing abuse.* New York, NY: Putnam Adult.

Bancroft, L. (2015). *Daily wisdom for why does he do that? Encouragement for women involved with angry and controlling men.* New York, NY: Berkley Books.

Bancroft, L., & Silverman, J. (2002). *The batterer as parent: The impact of domestic violence on* family *dynamics.* Thousand Oaks, CA: Sage Publications.

Biro v. Prudential Ins. Co. of America, 57 N.J. 204 (1970), aff'g o.b. 110 N.J. 391 (App. Div. 1970).

Bonomi, A., Holt, V., Martin, D., & Thompson, R. (2006). Severity of intimate partner violence in occurrence and frequency of police calls. *Journal of Interpersonal Violence, 21*(10), 1354–1364.

Bow, J., & Boxer, P. (2003). Assessing allegations of domestic violence in child custody evaluations. *Journal of Interpersonal Violence, 18*(12), 1394–1410.

Campbell, J. (2005). Assessing dangerousness in domestic violence cases: History, challenges, and opportunities. *Criminology and Public Policy, 4*, 653–671.

Campbell, M., Jaffe, P., & Kelly, T. (2008). *What about the men? Finding effective strategies for engaging abusive men and preventing the reoccurrence or escalation of violence against women.* London, Canada: Centre for Research and Education on Violence against Women and Children.

Campbell, M., Neil, J., Jaffe, P., & Kelly, T. (2010). Engaging abusive men in seeking community intervention: A critical research & practice priority. *Journal of Family Violence, 25*(4), 413–422.

Carney, M., & Barner, J. (2012). Prevalence of partner abuse: Rates of emotional abuse and control. *Partner Abuse, 3*(3), 286–335.

Catteneo, L., & Goodman, L. (2005). Risk factors for reabuse in intimate partner violence: A cross-disciplinary critical review. *Trauma, Violence, and Abuse, 6,* 141–175.

Child Welfare Information Gateway. (2015). *Child abuse and neglect fatalities 2013: Statistics and interventions.* Available at: https://www.childwelfare.gov/pubPDFs/fatality.pdf

Corvo, K. (2006). Violence, separation, and loss in the families of origin of domestically violent men. *Journal of Family Violence, 21*(2), 117–125.

Cox, C., Kotch, J., & Everson, M. (2003). A longitudinal study of modifying influences in the relationship between domestic violence and child maltreatment. *Journal of Family Violence, 18*(1), 5–17.

Daubert v. Merrell Dow Pharmaceuticals, Inc. (on remand), 43 F.3d. 1311 (9th Cir. 1995).

Edleson, J. (2004). Should childhood exposure to adult domestic violence be defined as child maltreatment under the law? In P. G. Jaffe, L. L. Baker, & A. Cunningham (Eds.), *Protecting children from domestic violence: Strategies for community intervention* (pp. 8–29). New York, NY: Guilford Press.

Eisikovits, Z., & Band-Winterstein, T. (2015). Dimensions of suffering among old and young battered women. *Journal of Family Violence 30*(1), 49–62.

Faller, K. (2015). Forty years of forensic interviewing of children suspected of sexual abuse, 1974–2014: Historical benchmarks. *Social Sciences, 4*(1), 34–65.

Ferraro, K. (2008). Invisible or pathological? Racial statistics and violence against women of color. *Critical Sociology, 34*(2), 193–211.

Fleury-Steiner, R., Bybee, B., Sullivan, C., Belknap, J., & Melton, H. (2006). Contextual factors impacting battered women's intentions to reuse the criminal legal system. *Journal of Community Psychology, 34*(3), 327–342.

Forssell, A., & Cater, A. (2015). Patterns in child-father contact after parental separation in a sample of child witnesses to intimate partner violence. *Journal of Family Violence, 30*(3), 339–349.

Fox, A., & Zawitz, M. (1999). *Homicide trends in the United States.* Washington, DC: US Department of Justice, Bureau of Justice Statistics. Retrieved June 29, 2004. http://www.ojp.usdoj.gov/bjs/abstract/ipva99.htm

Frye v. United States, 293 F. 1013 (D.C. Cir. 1923).

Gillum, T. (2009). Improving services to African American survivors of IPV. *Violence Against Women, 15*(1), 57–80.

Goddard, C., & Bedi, G. (2010). Intimate partner violence and child abuse: A child-centered perspective. *Child Abuse Review, 19*(1), 5–20.

Gondolf, E. (2008). Outcomes of case management for African-American men in batterer counseling. *Journal of Family Violence, 23,* 173–181.

Gondolf, E. (2009). Implementing mental health treatment for batterer program participants: Interagency breakdowns and underlying issues. *Violence Against Women, 15*(6), 638–655.

Gondolf, E., & Heckert, A. (2003). Determinants of women's perceptions of risk in battering relationships. *Violence and Victims, 18,* 371–386.

Goodman, L., & Epstein, D. (2008). *Listening to battered women: A survivor-centered approach to advocacy, mental health, and justice.* Washington, DC: American Psychological Association.

Gould, J. W., & Lehrmann, D. (2002) Evaluating the probative value of child custody evaluations. *Juvenile and Family Court Journal, 53*(2), 17–30.

Graham-Bermann, S., & Perkins S. (2010). Effects of early exposure and lifetime exposure to intimate partner violence (IPV) on child adjustment. *Violence and Victims, 25*(4), 427–439.

Halket, M., Gormley, K., Mello, N., Rosenthal, L., & Mirkin, M. (2014). Stay with or leave the abuser? The effects of domestic violence victim's decision on attribution made by young adults. *Journal of Family Violence 29*(1), 35–49.

Horrill, K., & Berman, H, (2004). *Getting out and staying out: Issues surrounding a woman's ability to remain out of an abusive relationship.* London, Canada: Centre for Research on Violence against Women and Children.

Jaffe, P., & Crooks, C. (2005). *Understanding women's experiences parenting in the context of domestic violence: Implications for community and court-related service providers.* Washington, DC: Violence Against Women Online Resources.

Jaffe, P., Crooks, C., & Wolfe, D. (2003). Legal and policy responses to children exposed to domestic violence: The need to evaluate intended and unintended consequences. *Clinical Child and Family Psychology Review, 6*(3), 205–213.

Johnson, I. (2007). Victims' perceptions of police response to domestic violence incidents. *Journal of Criminal Justice, 35*(5), 498–510.

Kennedy, A., Bybee, D, Sullivan, C., & Greeson, M. (April 2010). The impact of family and community violence on children's depression trajectories: Examining the interactions of violence exposure, family social support, and gender. *Journal of Family Psychology, 24*(2), 197–207.

Kitzmann, K., Gaylord, N., Holt, A., & Kenny, E. (2003). Child witnesses to domestic violence: A meta–analytic review. *Journal of Consulting and Clinical Psychology, 71*(2), 339–352.

Klein, A., Centerbar, D., Keller, S., & Klein, J. (2014). *The impact of differential sentencing severity for domestic violence and all other offenses over abusers' life spans.* Report to National Institute of Justice, U.S. Department of Justice, NCJ 244757. Available at: https://www.ncjrs.gov/pdffiles1/nij/grants/244757.pdf

Klevens, J., Baker, C., Shelley, G., & Ingram, E. (2008). Exploring the links between components of coordinated community responses and their impact on contact with intimate partner violence services. *Violence Against Women,* 14(3), 346–358.

Knight, C. (2006). Groups for individuals with traumatic histories: Practice considerations for social workers. *Social Work,* 51(1), 20–30.

Kropp, P. R. (2008). Intimate partner violence risk assessment and management. *Violence and Victims,* 23(2), 202–220.

Landrigan v. Celotex Corp., 127 N.J. 404 (1992).

Lewin, L., Abdrbo, A., & Burant, C. (2010). Domestic violence in women with serious mental illness involved with child protective services. *Issues in Mental Health Nursing,* 31(2), 128–136.

Lindsay, S. (2007). Autobiographical memory, eyewitness reports, and public policy. *Canadian Psychology,* 48(2), 57–66.

Lyon, T., & Dente, J. (2012). Child witnesses and the Confrontation Clause. *Journal of Criminal Law & Criminology,* 102(4), 1181–1232.

Mears, D., & Visher, C. (2005). Trends in understanding and addressing domestic violence. *Journal of Interpersonal Violence,* 20(2), 204–211.

Meier, J. (2009). A historical perspective on parental alienation syndrome and parental alienation. *Journal of Child Custody,* 6, 232–257.

Meier, J. (2010). Getting real about abuse and alienation: A critique of Drozd and Olesen's decision tree. *Journal of Child Custody,* 7, 219–252.

Miller, J. (October 3, 2014). Josh Powell's family asks Utah judge to declare Susan Powell dead. *The Salt Lake City Tribune.* Available at: http://www.sltrib.com/news/justice/1659999-155/powell-susan-josh-trust-cox-family

Morrel, T., Dubowitz, H., Kerr, M., & Black, M. (2003). The effect of maternal victimization on children: A cross–informant study. *Journal of Family Violence,* 18(1), 29–41.

Motzkau, J. (2007). Matters of suggestibility, memory and time: Child witnesses in court and what really happened. *Qualitative Social Research,* 8(1).

Oates, R. K., Jones, D. P., Denson, D., Sirotnak, A., Gary, N., & Krugman, R. D. (2000). Erroneous concerns about child sexual abuse. *Child Abuse and Neglect,* 24, 149–157.

Parham v. J.R., 442 U.S. 584 (1979).

Patel, S., & Choate, L. (2014). Conducting child custody evaluations: Best practices for mental health counselors who are court-appointed as child custody evaluators. *Journal of Mental Health Counseling* 36(1), 18–30.

Rhodes, K., Cerulli, C., Dichter, M., Kothari, C., & Barg, F. (2010). "I didn't want to put them through that": The influence of children on victim decision-making in intimate partner violence cases. *Journal of Family Violence, 25*(5), 485–493.

Rigterink, T., Katz, L., & Hessler, D (2010). Domestic violence and longitudinal associations with children's physiological regulation abilities. *Journal of Interpersonal Violence, 25*(9), 1669–1683.

Sadusky, J. (2006). *Pretrial release conditions in domestic violence cases: Issues and context.* Minneapolis, MN: Battered Women's Justice Project. Retrieved from http://www.bwjp.org/files/bwjp/ articles/Pretrial_Release.pdf

Salazar, L., Emshoff, J., Baker, C., & Crowley, T. (2007). Examining the behavior of a system: An outcome evaluation of a coordinated community response to domestic violence. *Journal of Family Violence, 22,* 631–641.

Saunders, B., & Meinig, M. B. (2000). Immediate issues affecting long term family resolution in cases of parent–child sexual abuse. In R. M. Reece (Ed.), *Treatment of child abuse: Common ground for mental health, medical, and legal practitioners* (pp. 36–53). Baltimore, MD: The Johns Hopkins University Press.

Saunders, D. G. (2008). *Anger management.* In C. Renzetti & J. Edleson (Eds.). *Encyclopedia of interpersonal violence.* Thousand Oaks, CA: Sage Publications.

Saunders, D. G. (2011). *Child custody evaluators' beliefs about domestic abuse allegations: Their relationship to evaluator demographics, background, domestic violence knowledge and custody-visitation recommendations.* Washington, D.C.: National Institute of Justice.

Stark, E. (2007). *Coercive control: The entrapment of women in personal life.* New York, NY: Oxford University Press.

State v. Kelly, 97 N.J. 178, 210 (1984); N.J. R. Evid. 702, Note 3.

State v. Harvey, 151 N.J. 117, 168 (1997).

State v. Marcus, 294 N.J. Super. 267, 275 (App. Div. 1996), *cert denied* 157 N.J. 543 (1998).

Suanez v. Egeland, 353 N.J. Super. 191, 195 (App. Div. 2002).

Tjaden, P., & Thoennes, N. (2000). *Extent, nature, and consequences of intimate partner violence.* Washington, D.C.: National Institute of Justice. Available at: https://www.ncjrs.gov/pdffiles1/nij/181867.pdf

Trocme, N., & Bala, N. (2005). False allegations of abuse and neglect when parents separate. *Child Abuse & Neglect, 29,* 1333–1345.

Vagianos, A. (February 13, 2015). 30 shocking domestic violence statistics that remind us it's an epidemic. The Huffington Post. Available at: http://www. huffingtonpost.com/2014/10/23/domestic-violence-statistics_n_5959776. html?fb_comment_id=fbc_712027705549924_712112732208088_ 712112732208088#f2ef86220c

Walker, L. (2009). *The battered woman syndrome* (3rd ed.). New York, NY: Springer.

Walker, L., & Shapiro, D. (2010). Parental alienation disorder: Why label children with a mental disorder? *Journal of Child Custody, 7*(4), 266–286.

Wolfe, D., Crooks, C., Lee, V., McIntyre-Smith, A., & Jaffe, P. (2003). The effects of children's exposure to domestic violence: A meta-analysis and critique. *Clinical Child and Family Psychology Review, 6*(3), 171–187.

Zweig, J., & Burt, M. (2006). Predicting case outcomes and women's perceptions of the legal system's response to domestic violence and sexual assault. *Criminal Justice Policy Review, 17*(2), 202–233.

INDEX

173